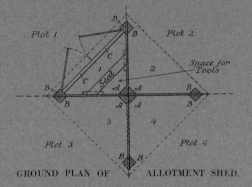

Plot 1

Plot 2

Space for
Tools

Plot 3

Plot 4

GROUND PLAN OF ALLOTMENT SHED.

THE GLORY OF THE GARDEN

A HORTICULTURAL CELEBRATION

✳

FROM THE PAGES OF

COUNTRY LIFE

THE GLORY OF THE GARDEN

A HORTICULTURAL CELEBRATION

FROM THE PAGES OF

COUNTRY LIFE

COUNTRY LIFE EDITOR MARK HEDGES

COMPILED AND EDITED BY SAM CARTER & KATE GATACRE
SERIES CONSULTANT JOHN GOODALL

SIMON &
SCHUSTER
ILLUSTRATED

London · New York · Sydney · Toronto · New Delhi

A CBS COMPANY

First published in Great Britain by Simon & Schuster UK Ltd, 2012
A CBS COMPANY

Copyright © 2012 *Country Life* Magazine

1 3 5 7 9 10 8 6 4 2

SIMON & SCHUSTER
ILLUSTRATED BOOKS
Simon & Schuster UK Ltd
222 Gray's Inn Road
London
WC1X 8HB

www.simonandschuster.co.uk

Simon & Schuster Australia, Sydney

Simon & Schuster India, New Delhi

Series Editor and Project Manager: Sam Carter
Series Consultant: John Goodall
Country Life Picture Library Manager: Justin Hobson
Designer: Two Associates/Richard Proctor
Literary Agent: Jonathan Conway, Mulcahy Conway Associates

A CIP catalogue record for this book is available from the British Library

ISBN 978-1-84983-765-1

Printed and bound by CPI Group (UK) Ltd, Croydon, CR0 4YY

CONTENTS

"The Englishman has a genuine
and deep-seated instinct for
making a garden"

Country Life, 1931

FOREWORD

It is as well, now and again, to admit that we're an odd lot. We gardeners, that is. We are compounded of a unique blend of patience, fatalism, boastfulness (when our vegetables are especially plump) and rivalry (when our vegetables are not as plump as our neighbour's), but above all we do what we do – in the main – because we like to feel we are improving things; making life a little more beautiful than it would otherwise be.

Real gardeners – those who grow things – are also, in my experience, unfailingly generous, as these contributions that have been made to *Country Life* over the last century prove. If we find a technique that works, we pass it on (unless it is a way of making our vegetables more plump, in which case until our showing days are over it is as well to be silent on the matter).

But champion vegetable growers apart, gardeners are not as a race competitive. Triumphs and tragedies are to be shared, for the common good. Oh, it might sound a touch altruistic, but then good gardeners are. What astonishes me about the contributions found within these pages is their variety, their brevity and the unlikeliness of some of their subjects. Ian Fleming, the creator of James Bond, when asked how to write a good thriller said: "You must keep your reader wanting to turn the page". *The Glory of the Garden* fulfils that brief. Not that I would claim it is a thriller, but just like James Bond's escapades it is a real eye-opener.

I know of no other book where information can be found on The Giant Gooseberry Business and The Electrification of Seeds; where you can discover how to make Musical Flower Pots, the secrets of Teaching Schoolboys to Love Trees or A Cure for Ivy Poisoning. If you can resist reading pieces entitled Statues for Bullets or Allotment Sheds for the

Unemployed then you are not the sort of person I hope to find myself sitting next to at the dinner table.

But what you hold in your hand is not merely a bran-tub of horticultural oddities. Within these pages are Gertrude Jekyll's plans for a blue border, thumbnail sketches of the "grand old man of gardening" William Robinson and the intrepid plant collector George Forrest – the botanical Indiana Jones of his day.

There are useful tips on controlling a range of pests and diseases (though some of the techniques used might make your eyes water), planting a carriage drive (well, you never know…) and rooftop gardening. In short, you will find yourself at one with Mr. Kipling when he opines that "the glory of the garden lies in more than meets the eye". Exactly the same could be said of *Country Life*.

ALAN TITCHMARSH

MARCH 2012

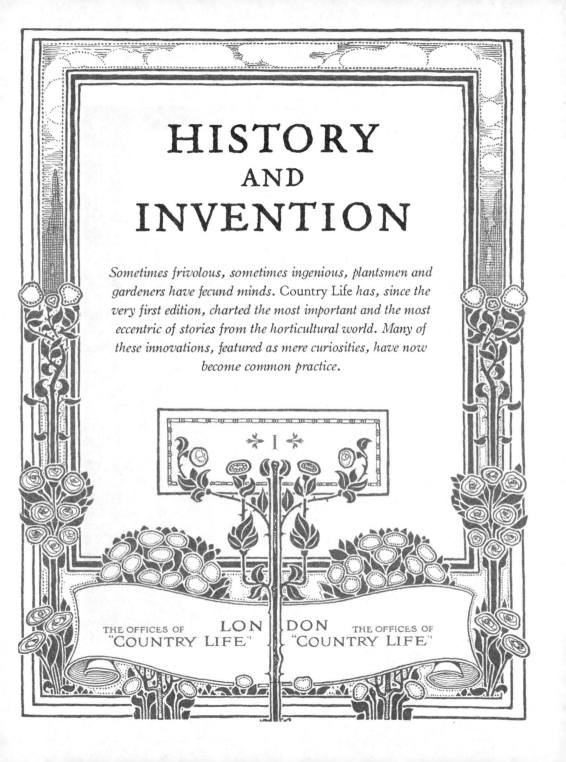

HISTORY
AND
INVENTION

Sometimes frivolous, sometimes ingenious, plantsmen and gardeners have fecund minds. Country Life has, since the very first edition, charted the most important and the most eccentric of stories from the horticultural world. Many of these innovations, featured as mere curiosities, have now become common practice.

I

THE OFFICES OF **LONDON** THE OFFICES OF
"COUNTRY LIFE" "COUNTRY LIFE"

SEPTEMBER 14ᵀᴴ, 1949

MUSICAL FLOWER POTS

The wonderfully named Sheldon Peach is delighted with his musical invention. The pot-bells, sadly, are rarely played today.

TO THE EDITOR OF "COUNTRY LIFE."

SIR,—In the spring of last year, while distributing geraniums and other potted plants, my trowel struck a medium-sized pot, giving out a very pleasing and decided tone. "Ah!" said I. "So this is what you can do!"

Striking again with a tender touch, the bell-like resonance so pleased me that I said to myself, "Why not some of your acquaintances, too?"

As my examination proceeded, it became quite fascinating to hear the ring of other pots of varied sizes, some of sufficient quality to merit distinction. I fixed the tonic (note C) and found I had one, two, three, four of scale upwards, so C, D, E, F. For most tunes, you need notes below the tonic – the National Anthem, for instance – but it was only the next day, by lifting various growing plants

"THE LAST TO BE FOUND WAS THE C SHARP"

and replacing them in the pots rejected upon music grounds, that I was able to find a perfect scale. Even then I was not satisfied, as many tunes require semitones, so I had to go on searching. The last to be found was the C sharp.

Your readers may be interested to know that all but one came from my own garden, and the pots are uncleaned, unaltered, and exactly as when in use. This is my pot-bells' second season.—SHELDON PEACH

NOVEMBER 7TH, 1925

THE EFFECT OF SMOKE ON PLANT LIFE

Country Life, characteristically, was loath to feature the dark satanic mills of industrial Britain. Here, however, the magazine provides an alarming account of the effects of smoke and smog on plants.

COAL SMOKE OFTEN affects the colour of flowers and, as a rule, the greater the pollution the paler the tint. The scarlet of the geranium in a smoke-infested area is often streaked with purple running to blue, while bronze-coloured flowers will frequently change to yellow.

According to Professor Cohen of Leeds, smoke from an industrial town will easily travel fifty miles or more – a worrying concern for nearby farmers and horticulturalists.

"EWES FED ON TURNIPS WERE NOT AFFECTED"

Orchid growers near London usually wash the outside of their orchid houses after every period of fog (last winter four times, at much cost). The deposit on the roofs is often so sticky from tar that soda has to be added to the water used for washing. Last winter quite fifty per cent of the choicest orchid blooms, including *cattleyas* and *laelio-cattleyas*, fell as a result of fog. The lack of light is also very detrimental to the health of the plants.

As for grass, Mr. James McDonald of Harpenden, one of the greatest authorities on grass in this country, tells me that in his opinion, "Fog and smoke have a distinctly harmful influence on grass. They cause a slimy scum and create an acidity which destroys the useful nitrifying bacteria in the soil. This, in turn, induces a coarse growth of grass and when rolling is done, as on a tennis court, weeds spring up at a rapid rate."

In a smoke-infested area, farmers find it difficult to provide adequate grazing for their animals. Dr. Ruston has kindly sent me some very interesting notes on the matter, in which he calls my attention to the high percentage of lambs lost in Yorkshire where the ewes were feeding on grass damaged by smoke. Ewes fed on turnips were not affected, however.

NOVEMBER 23RD, 1935

WATERING TREES

To the Editor of "Country Life."

Sir,—Your readers will no doubt be interested in the enclosed photograph, which shows an effective way of watering trees surrounded by concrete or paving. In this case it is a willow, which requires a damp soil. Although the concrete surrounds it considerably on three sides, a pipe of about 1 in. bore and 2 ft. long was placed vertically in the ground during planting, as far away as the concrete would allow. The water can be easily poured through using an ordinary watering can, and it extends down to the sandy soil, ensuring easy percolation. If the soil should be heavier, small stones or coarse gravel placed well round the bottom of the pipe should ensure the same result. When not in use, a plug or large cork prevents the entry of any solid matter.—T. Edmondson

[This method is useful for ensuring adequate moisture to any rather large shrub or young tree, and is particularly valuable when transplanting well-grown clipped yews. It is a variant of the more familiar "submerged flower-pot" method, by which a pot, buried up to its rim beside the shrub, is periodically filled with water.—Ed]

FEBRUARY 21ST, 1931

MODERN MOWING MACHINES

THERE IS NO more essential item than an efficient lawn mower. Although price is, naturally, an important factor, it is not one that should wholly govern the selection of a machine. The initial cost of a lawn mower is purely relative and must be considered in connection with the area of lawn to be mown and the state of the ground.

> "THERE IS NO MORE ESSENTIAL ITEM THAN AN EFFICIENT LAWN MOWER"

There has been an extraordinary advance made in lawn mower production during the last few years. A close study of the illustrated catalogues, and a frank discussion with those knowledgeable on the subject, should be made by those contemplating the purchase of a machine.—T.

MAY 1ST, 1926

THE NEW ROYAL HORTICULTURAL HALL

Country Life's architectural focus is here turned on the new Royal Horticultural Hall in Westminster. The building remains the headquarters of the RHS to this day.

THE EXISTING HALL in Vincent Square has for some years been regarded as inadequate, both for the Society's needs and from the point of view of exhibitors. A new and larger hall was therefore projected. Many sites were considered, but it was thought best to remain in the Westminster district, and the ultimate decision was to build on a site at the back of the existing hall. After seeing what was being done on the Continent, Messrs. Easton and Robertson produced the design for the new Horticultural Hall which is here illustrated.

> "THE EXISTING HALL HAS FOR SOME YEARS BEEN REGARDED AS INADEQUATE"

Light had to be carefully considered, and it is the construction and manner of the lighting of the hall which are the outstanding features of the design.

The construction will be in reinforced concrete, and it takes the form of a series of parabolic trusses rising to a height of about 66 ft., with tiers of vertical windows stepped up between them. This manner of lighting has been adopted for several new buildings on the Continent, but this is the first example of it to be carried out on a large scale in England.

Ordinarily, a great semicircular roof of an exhibition building is top-lighted, but the vertical system of lighting does not collect the dirt and soot of the city to the same extent, and any degree of shading can be obtained by means of blinds. The artificial lighting will be on a system employing colour screens, which will produce the effect of daylight.—R. R. P.

APRIL 13TH, 1901

TRANSPLANTING JOHN KNOX'S TREE

FINLAYSTONE HOUSE IS a hallowed spot to those who cherish the memory of John Knox. Under the tree on the famous lawn, the great reformer and preacher dispensed the sacrament of the Lord's Supper to his devoted followers. But the tree, a yew, was unfortunately in the way of modern improvements and had to be transplanted to another part of the grounds. It cannot be accused of possessing great beauty now, but it is pleasant to reflect that men like Mr.

> "THE MEN EMPLOYED BURROWED IN ALMOST A RABBIT FASHION"

G. F. Dickson – the current owner of Finlaystone House – cherish such trees not merely for their own sake, but for their historical associations.

The lifting was accomplished with consummate skill; this yew was no mere stripling but a heavy, cumbersome, and leafy tree, which without careful handling would have probably collapsed.

It may be of interest to those with great estates to know how the work was accomplished. Three large baulks of timber were first inserted beneath the ball of soil and roots. Considerable excavation of soil was necessary, and in the process of making an opening for the baulks, a sunken wall was discovered beneath the tree.

Inserting the baulks was certainly an arduous task – the men employed burrowing in almost a rabbit fashion, loosening the soil in advance and then scraping it out behind. Meanwhile, the trench along which the tree was to be dragged was being excavated.

When the baulks were in position, the root ball was completely detached from the surrounding soil, rollers were inserted under the baulks, and planks laid down to ensure the safe and easy removal of the heavy mass of roots and soil.

MAY 1ST, 1915

CHIMNEY POTS FOR ROSES

Undaunted by the naysaying of friends, relations and a landlord peu
sympathique, *a reader suggests an ingenious and economical solution
for producing blooms on a cement-covered verandah.*

TO THE EDITOR OF "COUNTRY LIFE."

SIR,—The following details may be of interest to those of your readers
who have experienced a similar difficulty to the one I describe. A bald
verandah confronted us, for the house we had taken was, being new,
quite bare. "When this is festooned with roses it will not look so bad,"
I exclaimed.

The landlord, a man who seldom agreed and was never agreeable,
overheard my remark. "You will spoil the verandah if you grow roses
over it," he said, "and whilst you may try, you will not succeed, for a bed
of concrete will hardly suit roses."

He was right – there was concrete for some distance round the pillars.

Soon after this conversation, I was visiting a pottery and noticed
many large chimney pots. Here was my opportunity. I ordered three to
be sent home immediately and had one placed by each pillar. They were
then filled with good soil and the roses Belle Lyonnaise, Gruss an Teplitz
and Alberic Barbier planted.

Friends and relations sneered, "How could roses grow without root
room?"

But with no more attention than frequent waterings, a little fresh soil
added occasionally, and a teaspoonful of Clay's Fertilizer administered
about once a month during spring and summer, grow they did. The
accompanying photograph gives but a little idea of the wonderful sheet
of intermingled blossoms that literally covered the roof of our verandah
last June. The aspect is due south, and the roses had been in their chimney
pots for four years.—E. BROUGHTON

MARCH 11TH, 1899

A NOVEL WAY OF GROWING STRAWBERRIES IN AMERICA

AN AMERICAN FARMER, Mr. J. P. Ohmer, of Dayton, Ohio, has discovered a novel way of growing strawberries which seems worthy of consideration. Our illustration shows this system of culture.

The plants are grown in large iron-bound barrels instead of beds. The barrels are set upon end, bored full of large holes in rows, and then filled with rich soil. The strawberry plants are set in the holes – one in each – and then all that remains to be given is a liberal supply of water at the roots.

"THREE OR FOUR BARRELS FILLED WITH PLANTS WOULD WELL SUPPLY AN ORDINARY FAMILY"

The fruits are much larger and finer than those from plants grown in beds, and Mr. Ohmer declares that each barrel produces half a bushel of strawberries in one season. The fruit is easily gathered, entirely free from sand or earth, and thoroughly ripened all round. The barrels are set 4 ft. apart, and an acre of land will hold 2,500 barrels, thus giving 1,250 bushels of strawberries to the acre. At this rate, three or four barrels filled with plants and set in a small kitchen garden would well supply an ordinary family.

OCTOBER 12TH, 1907

PLANT CULTURE BY ELECTRICITY

By B. H. Thwaite

Mr. Thwaite's idea of using electrical lighting to encourage the growth of vegetables is vital in today's production of vegetables.

THE Electric Culture Installation at the Royal Botanic Society's Gardens, Regent's Park, invented and patented by the writer, is attracting much attention. Briefly, it consists of an electro-static machine which discharges electricity at various points in the glasshouse to electrify not only the air, but the plants and their roots as well. The greenhouse is of the ordinary type of structure, some 50 ft. long by 16 ft. wide, and at the present moment it contains some 200 plants in pots, including geraniums, fuchsias and other popular flowering plants, as well as various kinds of grasses and palms, tomato plants, etc.

> "IT WILL REMOVE TO SOME EXTENT OUR DEPENDENCY DURING WINTER ON FOREIGN PRODUCTS"

Just below the roof of the house are two rails from which depend the arc lights, designed to secure as near an imitation as possible of natural solar effect. Directly the sun goes down, the arc lights are set in operation, moving automatically, constantly and almost imperceptibly along the entire length of the greenhouse. At the present time the plants are being given some three to four hours' additional artificial sunlight; should the weather be dull or fogs arise, the artificial rays would be given for a longer period. In a house close by there is to all intents and purposes a duplicate set of plants, by which it is possible to ascertain something of the effect of the artificial sunlight.

It is early to say definitely what a nurseryman adopting the system could hope to obtain, but strawberries, I imagine, could be ripened in seven weeks and raspberries and grapes in about two and a half months from shooting.

If the installation at Regent's Park succeeds in securing the results expected, it will remove to some extent our dependency during winter on foreign products, which obviously cannot bring with them the sweetness and flavour of those newly gathered.

JANUARY 3RD, 1920

THE ROLLING STEPS

To the Editor of "Country Life."

SIR,—The illustration shows a very useful garden appliance. Some double steps were bought at a country sale; they had been used for passing over a wire fence. With the help of a handy carpenter we had one side cut away and back legs added instead. The legs ended in a pair of small, strong wheels.

Handles like those of a wheelbarrow were bolted to both back and front, forming strong braces and a means of trundling it along like a barrow. A wider tread at the top gives good standing room.

The rolling steps enable a man to do the trimming of his big cypress hedge in comfort, and is useful for many other jobs of pruning and training.—G. J.

MAY 13TH, 1949

FOR COMBATING FROST

To the Editor of "Country Life."

Sir,—I recently visited America to study the latest applications of electricity to agriculture and horticulture, and have some data on the use of electric radiant heat lamps in orchards that may be of interest.

Although a number of such appliances have been made, their electrical loading is likely to be heavy – something of the order of 430 kw per acre – and it is doubtful whether such a load would be economical. They also provide questionable protection against severe frosts, and are expensive compared with oil heaters.

With all methods of radiant heating, there is the objection that those parts of the plants or trees not directly exposed to the radiant energy may not be protected. Even if this form of heating were suitable for open crops, it is doubtful whether it would be effective in orchards, owing to the screening effect of the trees.—F. E. ROWLAND

NOVEMBER 23RD, 1918

THE ELECTRIFICATION OF SEEDS: A REVOLUTION IN AGRICULTURE

BY CHARLES A. MERCIER

SEED CORN CAN now be electrified. It is a simple process, easily performed, occupying only a few hours, and no more difficult than the process of dyeing a parcel of yarn or sterilising a surgical dressing. The grain, steeped in salty water (calcium or sodium salt, depending on the soil to be used), is exposed to electricity in a large tank, the strength of the solution and of the current being altered as to the kind of seed (barley, wheat, or oats).

It is known that farmers are a cautious and conservative race, not eager to adopt new methods until these have been well tried at other people's risk and had their value proved beyond question. But quite enough is now known to prove that, if properly conducted, the process is of very great value and farmers – meeting at market and talking about the weather and their crops – have been discussing this at length, and positively.

In the first place, there is a notable increase in the yield of grain from electrified seed, exceeding that of the unelectrified by one to four sacks per acre, each sack containing 4 bushels.

This result alone justifies – nay, almost demands – the adoption of the process, but this is far from being the whole of the advantage.

The quality of the crop, as indicated by weight per bushel, is also improved, as is the length, stoutness and strength of the straw crop. And there seems to be a great likelihood that the process is protective against smut, bunt, rust and other fungus diseases; at any rate, the treatment does not increase the plant's susceptibility to such things.

> "FARMERS ARE A CAUTIOUS AND CONSERVATIVE RACE"

The advantage accruing from the process is not uniform: we cannot say beforehand whether the crop will be greatly benefited or only moderately benefited. All we can say is that it will be benefited.

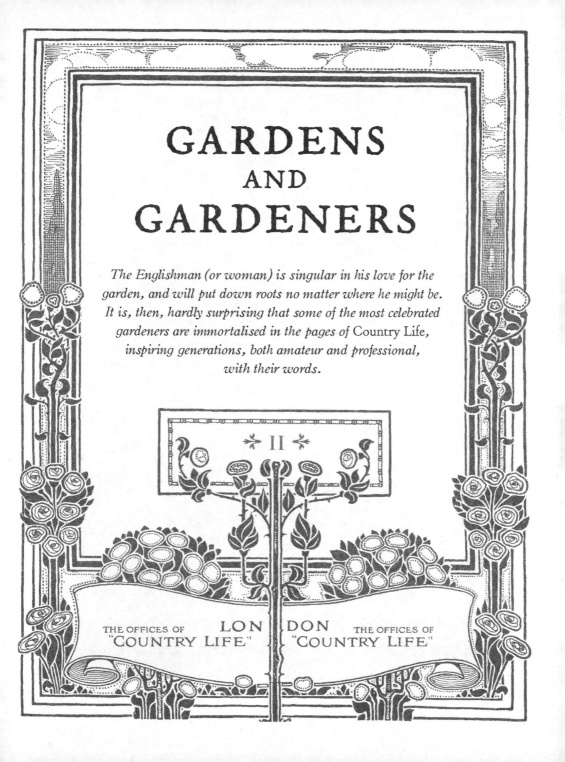

GARDENS
AND
GARDENERS

The Englishman (or woman) is singular in his love for the garden, and will put down roots no matter where he might be. It is, then, hardly surprising that some of the most celebrated gardeners are immortalised in the pages of Country Life, inspiring generations, both amateur and professional, with their words.

❖ II ❖

THE OFFICES OF LONDON THE OFFICES OF
"COUNTRY LIFE" "COUNTRY LIFE"

FARRER'S INTRODUCTIONS TO OUR GARDENS

A SHORT SURVEY
BY M. COX

REGINALD FARRER DIED just five years ago, on October 16th, 1920, at Nyitadi, on the Burmese–Chinese frontier. There is no need to recall for British gardeners Farrer's work as a writer, for the popularity of his books remains unabated. There has probably been no writer on matters connected with gardens who produced such a vivid picture of the plants about which he wrote. He had his likes and dislikes, and did not hesitate to press them home by every means at his facile brain's disposal, but behind

> "BEHIND ALL WAS A GREAT LOVE OF PLANTS AND AN UNDERSTANDING OF THEIR CHARMS AND IDIOSYNCRASIES"

all was a great love of plants and an understanding of their charms and idiosyncrasies. There is no doubt that his books will retain their deserved popularity for many years to come.

Prior to 1913 he made constant trips to the Alps – a broad term which includes the Dolomites – and his finds are recorded in some of his earlier books like *Among the Hills* and *The Dolomites*. In these he not only describes new forms, which ultimately found a place in his gardens at Ingleborough, but also old favourites with which most of his readers were acquainted. In this way he carried his readers with him to well-remembered nooks in the high hills.

AUGUST 4TH, 1917

A DESERT GARDEN

To the Editor of "Country Life."

Sir,—The first job when Private Bird with his Bedouin helpers commenced to cultivate this oasis in the Libyan desert was breaking up the ground which had been lying idle and trampled by many feet for over a year. Bird's feelings can be imagined when he saw his new hands tackle the job in a sitting position with small mattocks. They cast aside the shovels and spades provided for them as "mush quies" – no good – and they carried out the work in the same manner and with the same tools as used in the days of Christ.

> "PRIVATE BIRD WITH HIS BEDOUIN HELPERS COMMENCED TO CULTIVATE THIS OASIS IN THE LIBYAN DESERT"

As Bird remarked, "They was a bit of a shock to me at first, but I do see now they knows what they're about. They're pretty good workmen, considering all things, and I lets 'em go their own way."

The next thing to do was to run the water channels from the various small wells over the garden, and this they carried out entirely by eye, merely scraping a channel here and raising a small embankment or aqueduct of soil there, and when the water was pumped up it ran level through the garden. The average Englishman would have spent two days arriving at the levels with instruments, and then would have been hopelessly at fault in a dozen places, but these uneducated Bedouins hit off the lie of the land exactly, using the most haphazard methods.—S. J.

MAY 14ᵀᴴ, 1932

MISS GERTRUDE JEKYLL

BY E. V. LUCAS

"GOD FIRST PLANTED a garden" – we know that on the authority of Lord Bacon. But of the assiduity and methods of the first lady gardener we know little. How long a step it is from Eve to Miss Gertrude Jekyll no one can say: the evolutionists and the bishops are still at variance. I am satisfied, however, that in the history of women in horticulture, Miss Jekyll was a true pioneer.

> "NEXT TO THE CREATOR, NO ONE HAS DONE SO MUCH AS GERTRUDE JEKYLL TO MAKE ENGLAND A BEAUTIFUL COUNTRY"

Before Miss Jekyll there had been William Robinson, whose great books, *The English Flower Garden* and *The Wild Garden*, laid emphasis on the importance of letting Nature have a hand in the disposition of plants. But it was Miss Jekyll, in *Wood and Garden*, published in 1899, who revolutionised the gardener's art and killed the old stiff fashions of bedding.

She writes: "I am strongly for treating garden and wooded ground in a pictorial way . . . and for so arranging plants and trees and grassy spaces that they look happy and at home, and make no parade of conscious effort . . . A garden so treated gives the delightful feeling of repose, and refreshment."

In the days when her activity was greater, Miss Jekyll used to go all over the country to give advice as to the laying out of gardens, and it was not only the rich who commanded her energy. Her heart has always been large enough to extend sympathy and helpfulness to everyone with a genuine appeal.

MAY 18ᵀᴴ, 1935

WILLIAM ROBINSON

IN MR. WILLIAM ROBINSON, who died on Sunday at the age of ninety-six, the "grand old man" of English gardening has passed away. In order to realise how he changed the face of gardening, it is necessary to look back to Victorian days. Although it is the habit nowadays, perversely or otherwise, to admire much that was Victorian, the Victorian garden could never be praised according to modern tenets. The Victorian gardener was unimaginative in his use of plants outside – tightly tied by the apron strings of convention, and inexpressibly conservative. He loved strong, garish colours in serried ranks, and everything was meticulous and neat; he abhorred the natural and the unconventional.

"TO SWEEP AWAY THE SHRUBBERIES OF BAY AND LAUREL – THOSE SOUR, DANK WILDERNESSES"

William Robinson, however, was the antithesis of the Victorian gardener. Robinson loved the herbaceous border which had been neglected for fifty years and wanted to sweep away the shrubberies of bay and laurel – those sour, dank wildernesses. He was fully aware of the natural beauty of flowering trees and shrubs that were rarely seen, and above all did he visualise the beauty of the woodland glade, thinned and decked with flowers, that became part and parcel of the scene.

As well as being a practical gardener of the first quality, he was also a skilled writer. His books abound with common sense. He founded three journals: *The Garden*, *Gardening Illustrated*, and *The Flora and Sylva*.

During the last twenty-five years of his life Robinson was a cripple, but in his wheeled chair he continued to take as close an interest as ever in every plant – almost in every tree – at his Sussex home. It is pleasant to be able to add that the last words he wrote were an introduction to a book on Clematis by his head gardener, Mr. Ernest Markham, shortly to be published by COUNTRY LIFE.

In William Robinson the garden world has lost a figure who cannot be replaced until a practical gardener, skilled with his pen, of indomitable and pugnacious energy, evolves yet another complete system of gardening related to modern architecture – if such a thing is conceivable.

JANUARY 23RD, 1932

A GREAT PLANT COLLECTOR

GARDENERS ALL OVER the world will have learned with deep regret, and a sense of personal loss, of the untimely death of Mr. George Forrest, the well-known plant collector, at Tengyueh, a little over a fortnight ago. Mr. Forrest was just preparing to return home after completing his seventh plant-hunting trip to the Far East. His death is a real loss to horticulture and botany for, although his work in the field was nearing its close, there was much awaiting his attention at home, including the identification and classification of his many discoveries.

Since his first expedition to Yunnan in 1904, to collect for Mr. A. K. Bulley, at the instigation of the late Sir Isaac Bayley Balfour of the Royal Botanic Garden, Edinburgh, he has collected some 30,000 plant specimens, which include well over a thousand plants new to science, and has been responsible for the reintroduction of many plants that had been previously introduced by such collectors as Delavay but had, over time, been lost to cultivation. Although interested in every kind of plant, he was undoubtedly a specialist in the two enormous genera of rhododendrons and primulas. His introductions were so numerous and so varied that it is impossible even to attempt a list, but it is safe to say that many of the finest of our garden plants are the result of his labours in the field.

In addition to plants, he made large and important collections of birds, insects, moths and butterflies on his expeditions, and has added enormously to our knowledge of the natural history of the mountainous country around the Mekong and Salween rivers.

No European knew more of the province of Yunnan and the Chino-Tibetan borderland – its flora and fauna, and its people – than Forrest, and no one was held in higher esteem by the inhabitants and by his own band of native collectors. No difficulty, danger or hardship was too great for him to overcome in pursuit of his work, as those who have heard him tell of his hairbreadth escapes on his earlier expeditions in 1904 and 1910 will know. He has died, as he doubtless would have wished, among the hills he loved so well. He has left a rich heritage for all who love and grow plants, and his name is perpetuated in many of his discoveries, of which *Primula Forrestii, Pieris Forrestii, Buddleia Forrestii* and *Iris Forrestii* are but a few of the more outstanding examples.

APRIL 29TH, 1916

GARDENING AS A WOMAN'S PASTIME

By Gertrude Jekyll

GARDENING, IN ALL but the rougher mechanical processes, is essentially work for women: the infinite detail, the varied manipulation, and the need for unceasing watchfulness and sympathy, are all matters that appeal to them keenly and closely. And it is especially those who are the better born, whose earlier years have been tenderly guarded and in whose case class convention has stood in the way of any idea of manual labour, who now find that in the actual contact with the soil, in the getting down to close intimacy with Nature, the hitherto closed door to a whole new world of interest and delight and fruitful understanding has been opened to them.

> "THE INFINITE DETAIL, THE VARIED MANIPULATION, AND THE NEED FOR UNCEASING WATCHFULNESS"

Splendid health, strength of body and limb, quickened intellect, and joy of life tenfold increased – these are the added rewards of what in itself is the happiest and wholesomest way of life that anyone can desire.

Now, especially, there must be many young women, daughters of clergymen, of officers in the Army and Navy, and others whose means of living have been straitened by the costs and burdens occasioned by the war, who must be facing the need of preparing themselves for some means of earning their own livelihood. Let any of those who should decide on making gardening their business rejoice in the prospect of two years of student life, full of interest, health and enjoyment.

NOVEMBER 25TH, 1933

HENRY AVRAY TIPPING

BY CHRISTOPHER HUSSEY

IN HENRY AVRAY TIPPING, COUNTRY LIFE loses its oldest and most valued contributor. It was in 1907 that he began to contribute those articles on country houses which, during the course of twenty-five years, provided him and COUNTRY LIFE with the material for the well-known series of volumes on English Homes which will constitute a lasting memorial to him.

But his real love was, of course, the garden. As a young man he was one of that small band of enthusiasts who gathered round Mr. Robinson and Miss Jekyll in their crusade for natural planting against the wearisome "bedding out" practised in the 1870s and 1880s. In the long campaign between the advocates of the wild and those of the revived formal garden – the latter led by Sir Reginald Blomfield – he adopted, from the first, that middle course which common sense dictated and which has become the accepted view today. In this he was guided by his historical knowledge no less than by instinctive taste, and in the late Harold Peto he had a friend with similar views. If he only had behind him the series of gardens that he made for himself between 1888 and the present day, even excluding those that he so much enjoyed laying out for his friends, he would have won for himself an honourable place among those who, during the past half-century, have given English gardening the leading place it occupies today in the Western world.

"He reminded one of a fallen tree," a friend said of Henry during his last illness. To talk with him then, still fully dressed and vigorous of mind, though painfully weak, was indeed to be reminded of some hedge-row giant laid low, seen to be all the greater for its proneness. Whether as gardener, savant, or friend, it was above all his generous zest that infected all who had to do with him and will long keep his memory green and deep-trenched in their hearts.

A PERSONAL RECOLLECTION

By Lady Congreve

ENRY AVRAY TIPPING was twenty-two, and I a little girl of eleven, when we first met, and we have been friends for fifty-six years. His father was squire of the parish where my stepfather was rector.

He was a living contradiction of the saying "Jack of all trades, master of none," for he was certainly master of everything he undertook. But first and last came his love of gardening, and I think I understand what it meant to him. His own gardens were not the sort that have to be run by dozens of gardeners. A weed was not a crime, and in autumn he liked the leaves to lie about until they were all down. But in planning great masses and stretches of colour for all seasons of the year he had no rival. And he did not love flowers only in bulk; he loved each one individually. He always held a flower as if he loved it.

JANUARY 22ND, 1943

RATIONING GARDENERS

There is a whole world of social history to be found within Country Life. *Here a plea for a "pool" of scarce wartime gardeners in the correspondence pages meets with a cool response from another reader.*

TO THE EDITOR OF "COUNTRY LIFE."

SIR,—Nowadays there are very few gardeners left, these being part-time, old men and a few boys, but they are needed desperately by certain people who are doing their best to grow vegetables but who are not really strong enough to do the heavy digging.

At the moment it is sheer luck who manages to get any help, but it is certainly maddening to see those lucky few who can manage to get a gardener still keeping up their pre-war flowers and immaculate lawns. Certainly let us have a few flower gardens, but it does seem wrong to employ all the labour for the purpose. If people want their flowers as a healthful hobby then they should do the work themselves.

> "IT IS MADDENING TO SEE THOSE LUCKY FEW WHO CAN MANAGE TO GET A GARDENER STILL KEEPING UP THEIR PRE-WAR FLOWERS AND IMMACULATE LAWNS"

It would seem only fair for each town and village to have a pool of gardeners and for them to be allowed to work only for those who need them for food growing. These part-time gardeners would give many people a much-needed hand and, of course, once you have started off growing your own vegetables, you're caught for life!—ELIZABETH CROSS, TUDOR HOUSE, SELSEY, SUSSEX

SIR,—Your correspondent from Selsey (January 22nd) answers herself in her letter, as no good gardener could work always at heavy work without seeing his plants through all stages. Pooled gardeners would only get the nasty jobs and would have a poor time. Your correspondent evidently does not know that good gardeners take pride in their gardens and will see that their lawns and beds are well kept, even if it means much extra effort.

> "THEY WOULD NOT MIND BEING 'TOLD' – A THING THAT SOME GARDENERS HATE..."

I have had no difficulty in getting gardeners, and there is also no shortage of boys for the cruder work.

Also, being somewhat inexperienced, they would not mind being "told" – a thing that some gardeners hate.—SUSSEX

MAY 28TH, 1932

TEACHING SCHOOLBOYS
TO LOVE TREES

To the Editor of "Country Life."

Sir,—I was visiting, on Sunday, a well-known preparatory school in this neighbourhood, Huyton Hill School, near Knowsley Park, and found that each of the boys is asked to contribute a young tree to their "Tree Library". This seemed to me such a good idea for training the young to know and love trees – especially in Lancashire, where our trees have to put up such a hard fight against the smoky atmosphere. Each boy plants his own tree, and his name, the name of the tree, and the date are branded on an oak label which he has made himself in the school workshop.
—C. H. Reilly

JULY 14TH, 1900

A GARDENER'S CLAIM TO PLANTS

To the Editor of "Country Life."

Sir,—I dismissed my gardener, and on leaving he removed from my garden and greenhouse some 300 plants which he alleged were his property and had been brought upon the premises by him. I cannot prove that this was not so, but for some two or three years the plants have been grown in my pots and in my soil, and have been tended by labour for which I have paid, and I contend that the plants consequently became my property. I believe that a similar case was decided a few months ago, and against the same gardener. Can you help me to trace it, as it might form a valuable precedent for my own case, and might be useful to many of your readers?—Alpha

[Unfortunately we do not remember this particular case, and as it is probable no question of law was raised, perhaps the case has not been reported in any of the legal papers. The question raised would be one of fact, and it may be as well to point out that, although there is a natural presumption that plants which have been growing for two or three years in a garden or greenhouse belong to the owner of the premises, they are not necessarily his property. But if any other person claims them as his, that person must strictly prove his claim. Your gardener must therefore prove that the plants were his own property when brought upon your premises. If that is established, you must then prove, not necessarily by direct evidence, that the ownership was subsequently changed.—Ed]

THINGS ABOUT OUR NEIGHBOURHOOD

When you go to this much trouble to mix the perfect medium for your roses, a paragon such as Bingle the gardener is essential.

BINGLE IS OUR present gardener, a medium-sized, loosely-hung, fair man, with eyes the colour of *Myosotis palustris "semperflorens"*. He told father that he "believed he was a Christian," and had begun life as dog-boy to the squire. I have since learned that as a lad, the nastiest job Bingle was ever put to was picking the gentles out of carcases that were hung up for weeks and weeks to feed the young pheasants with.

> "WHAT I LIKE ABOUT BINGLE IS THAT HE DOES NOT ARGUE. ARGUMENT IS INTOLERABLE IN A GARDEN"

What I like about Bingle is that he does not argue. Argument is intolerable in a garden. He surveys the preparation of my tea rose beds with a funereal air. Indeed our four-foot holes and the barrow-loads of chalk we took out had some resemblance to the digging of graves in an upland churchyard.

The Reservist would have reasoned with me about my broken bricks, my layer of hazel boughs, and my rough turf. The joy of mixing the compost would have been ruined for me; as it was, I revelled in it. Bingle and I

THINGS ABOUT OUR NEIGHBOURHOOD

cleared a great space in the manure yard and sifted six barrow-loads of rotted turf mould, six of a dry black mud I got leave to cart from an old pond, six of sharp road scrapings, and to this we added the fibre from the turf and four loads of short manure. Finally, I ventured four loads of dried and sifted red clay, and the whole was evenly spaded to a centre by two men. That was then wheeled into the rose garden, tipped into the holes, and the entire pie recommenced.

Thus we made six beds: each was 4 ft. deep and about 5 ft. square. Filled with this concentrated food, they were allowed to sink all summer, and carried meantime the finest *Salpiglossis* ever seen in these parts. In autumn they were filled up, roughed over, and frosted, and in February six sorts of teas were bought and ten plants of a kind put in each bed. The delight of doing things in the real way, as one is so seldom allowed to do them!

MARCH 29TH, 1941

EVACUEES' GARDENS

The joys of introducing town children to growing their own vegetables – a most useful pastime during the war years. The suggested Christmas present, however, might appear somewhat lacking in festive cheer to modern sensibilities.

TO THE EDITOR OF "COUNTRY LIFE."

SIR,—Let us hope that the evacuees now living in country districts will do all they can this spring to help in the production of vegetables. Our own evacuees, whom we have had with us since the beginning of the war, had each a small garden patch given them last year where they raised potatoes and vegetables. Though the work needed a good deal of supervision, it was of great interest to them and of much educational value. When their parents came from town to visit them, the boys were able to give them parcels of fresh vegetables to take home. At Christmas time there was a sack of potatoes under the Christmas tree – an evacuee's present to his grandmother who had come out to the party. What pride and satisfaction! Let us hope that next season's crops will be even better.— EVACUEES' HOSTESS

JUNE 29TH, 1940

THE ODD-MAN

As the war challenged old certainties, Country Life *felt obliged to provide some very useful advice on how to handle the new and necessary character of the odd-job man with tact.*

BE IT THIS year, next year, sometime – life, as we knew it, will be ended. Failing a sudden increase of insanity, still more of our country houses will stand empty – forlorn reminders of happier days. The market garden may absorb some of those acres of kitchen garden and glass-houses, but the head gardener will soon be a rarity, and the Odd-Man will reign in his stead. I do not deny that the species of Odd-Man has existed sporadically for years. Bred perhaps in Ireland, and fostered by the Church of England, he is one whose popularity during the "war to end war" increased a hundred-fold.

It is no small task trying to adapt a garden that has been tended by several minions to one pair of hands, and those not constant. Some give up the struggle altogether, saying that they "do so like a wild garden – have you ever been to Wisley?" But with a little thought and a hardening of heart at times, it is possible to make such a garden, if not the riot of colour of the catalogue, at least reasonably interesting from spring. The Odd-Man needs tactful handling, and it is a help if one recognises from the outset that there are mountains that no faith will move. Bedding-out, in the strict sense, is an impossibility, and here considerable opposition may be encountered from the Odd-Man. He will cling to his *Calceolarias*, his *Lobelia*, and an unpleasant foliage plant with leaves of many-coloured blotting-paper. If the beds must remain, Poulsen roses, once planted, will give months of colour with a minimum of attention.

No plant is easier to grow than the June-flowering iris, but the Odd-Man will have views about it that must be eradicated firmly if kindly. —A. C. B.

MARCH 17TH, 1917

OUR GARDENERS

BY ALFRED OLLIVANT

THREE MEN WORKED here before the war. Now the place of the three men has been taken by one boy and two goats. We bought them – the goats, I mean – in June at six weeks of age. It was the woman's idea. Flushed with triumph, she came back from the village one evening to announce what she had done – our fortunes were made! She had paid Mr. Trewen, our neighbour the butcher, 5s. apiece for two kids, and would I give her the money for them?

They should do the garden all the summer, labour being short, and next spring they should have kids of their own. We should sell the kids at a great profit, while the nannies would give their milk to our little daughter. When they were not giving milk to Rachel, they would be taking her out in a go-cart, and when they were too old to either give milk or take the family to church, we should sell them back to Mr. Trewen for purposes the woman thought it unnecessary to specify. It was a great scheme.

The goats proved a disappointment, and some time later I asked Mr. Trewen for 10s. apiece for them. He offered me 7s. 6d. Knowing the exact worth of the goats, I took the money with an outwardly sullen and grudging air, as of one who says, "I am being done down and I know it," but inwardly I was gleeful. That was some days since, and I notice that Mr. Trewen has not yet come to fetch his treasures. They are still grazing on the lawn beside their tubs and bumping their empty heads together, playing at war instead of taking a noble if unpretentious part in it.

"When they were not giving milk to Rachel, they would be
taking her out in a go-cart."

APRIL 29TH, 1916

WOMEN AS GARDENERS

To the Editor of "Country Life."

Sir,—While fully concurring with your admirable remarks in Country Life on the occupation of gardening for women fond of open-air life and of fairly strong physique, may I point out that just that practical manual training which you advocate has for many years been given at the Swanley Horticultural College for Women. On the forty-three acres of the college training-grounds, the pupils themselves carry out all branches of manual work, from rolling, digging, sweeping and so forth to mending greenhouse roofs. The Swanley girl is amply trained to be a "handy woman" in all gardening operations. The teaching, of course, includes full scientific gardening, but my point at the moment only concerns the manual training given.

And may I add that the profession is in a more flourishing case than would, perhaps, appear from a careless reading of your notes. The demand at Swanley for trained women gardeners for salaried posts exceeds the supply. Can as much be said of any other profession for women? Of all past students, twenty-six are now engaged as head gardeners, thirteen as under-gardeners, eight as jobbing gardeners, and twenty-five as market gardeners. Eighteen are teaching in school gardens and, as five hundred and seventy elementary schools now have gardens, teachers for these are in steadily increasing demand. And during last year alone, seven Swanley students obtained posts as head gardeners, five as gardeners and under-gardeners, and six started work as market gardeners. If this is the record of one horticultural college for women, surely the outlook for the well-trained, practical woman gardener is full of encouragement.—G. M. Godden

DECEMBER 5ᵀᴴ, 1908

CHILDREN AND GARDENS

S A RULE, the children's gardens are poked away in some dismal corner where no plant will nor could attempt to grow, but which is, however, considered good enough for the little people to "spuddle" in. In fact, this is precisely one of those shams – accepted for the moment in child-like good faith – which after a short trial is quickly detected by the children themselves. It is self-evident how few of us have had the wit in the past to perceive that, in the words of Miss Jekyll, "It is neither fair nor reasonable to give a child who wishes for a garden a place that is full of difficulties," or have guessed that "to do so is to crush at the outset that latent healthy instinct which the good God has implanted in so many human hearts to be a joy and solace from youth to age."

"THE CHILDREN SHOULD WELL BE ALLOWED THE HAPPINESS AND EXCITEMENT OF BEGINNING IN THE MIDDLE"

Only an experienced gardener would advise the giving of the ready-made flower-plot into the children's keeping, rather than leaving the planning of it to the immature efforts of small hands. The elders have learned, probably hardly enough and through many delays and failures, the difficulties of "beginning at the beginning" in garden matters. The children should well be allowed the happiness and excitement of beginning in the middle of the one art in which it may be possible for exception to prove the rule.—K. L. D.

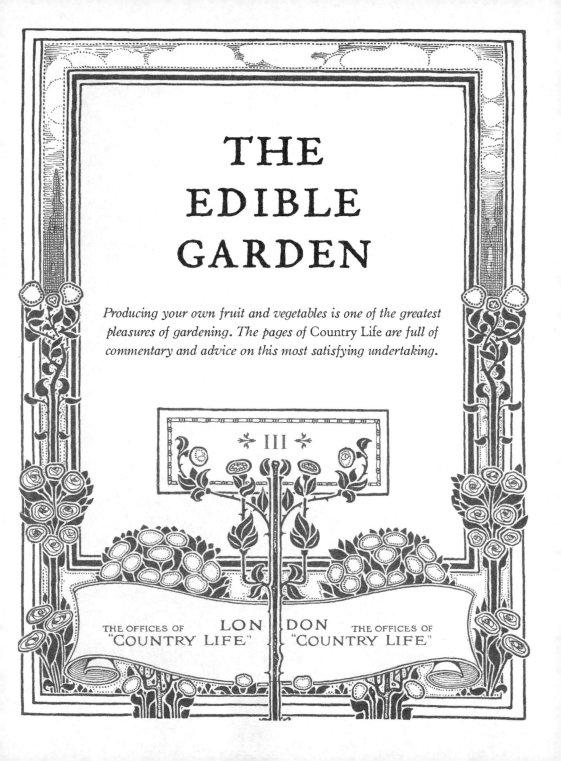

THE
EDIBLE
GARDEN

Producing your own fruit and vegetables is one of the greatest pleasures of gardening. The pages of Country Life *are full of commentary and advice on this most satisfying undertaking.*

III

THE OFFICES OF
"COUNTRY LIFE"

LON DON

THE OFFICES OF
"COUNTRY LIFE"

AUGUST 5TH, 1933

CULINARY HERBS

To the Editor of "Country Life."

Sir,—Of late years, probably owing to the increasing interest in flowers, the herb garden seems to have almost disappeared, and the demand for dried herbs is, to a large extent, now being met commercially. In the fen districts of Cambridgeshire, however, and at this period of the year, one can see fields upon fields of growing herbs.

Generally the herbs are cut and gathered by hand, and this provides employment for a large section of the female population. Immediately after cutting, the herbs are loaded into carts and taken to the adjacent factory. Here they are passed through an ingenious steam dryer, and eventually through special apparatus which removes the stalk and desiccates the leaves to the required size.

The whole process of drying is very expeditious – less than thirty minutes elapses between the green and the prepared states.

Finally they are put into packets and bottles by the deft fingers of girls, and eventually distributed to the retail trade.—Herbert G. Ayres

NOVEMBER 23RD, 1900

A HOUSE OF MUSCATS

A proud mother on her sons' success in growing the tricky Muscatel grape in Sussex and producing a valuable crop from the vines.

To the Editor of "Country Life."

Sir,—I enclose a photograph just taken of a fine crop of muscatel grapes grown by my sons at their fruit farm near Worthing, Sussex. The crop is an exceptionally fine one, the weight of grapes being roughly estimated at 2,000 lbs. The vines started naturally by sun heat one March, and were fit to cut at the beginning of September. They are now in their fourth year and this is their second crop. These grapes when forced early are known to fetch as much as 7s. 6d. a pound, wholesale. The ground and climate of Worthing is particularly suited to growing fruit of all descriptions, especially grapes, tomatoes and cucumbers. The muscatel is considered the most difficult species of grape to grow, as the fruits do not set well unless very skilfully managed. They are now a rich golden colour and simply exquisite in flavour.—Christine Douglas

DECEMBER 31ST, 1921

MARROWS IN SWITZERLAND

To the Editor of "Country Life."

Sir,—I hope you may care to see the marrows that are my pride and pleasure looking at the Swiss mountains among which they are grown.

"I AM NOW MUCH MORE INTERESTED IN MARROWS THAN IN MOUNTAINEERING"

I began to grow them six years ago, but never had such a good year as this one. I have raised three kinds, the heaviest one striped yellow and green, and the others plain dark green and plain light green respectively. I am now much more interested in marrows than in mountaineering.—W. H. WIDDICOMBE

JANUARY 13TH, 1940
CABBAGE HEARTS FOR SALADS

A Country Life *reader introduces "cold slaw" to England, as lettuces from the Continent were no longer available after the outbreak of World War II.*

TO THE EDITOR OF "COUNTRY LIFE."

SIR,—The absence of imported lettuces and the natural hiatus in their production in this country in midwinter has caused dismay to many who value the dietetic value of salads. Dietetic value is specially mentioned, as no real salad lover could compare the soft flab of a winter lettuce that has travelled far to the succulent crispness of those grown in the open garden during spring and summer. What is odd is that no one seems to have drawn attention to the excellent salad value of the white hearts of some cabbages and savoys, simply shredded and eaten raw. In many parts of the Continent this is a favourite and nutritious winter dish; it is also very popular in the United States, where it is served under the name of "Cold Slaw." In passing, it is as well to point out that this has nothing in common with pickled cabbage, a coarse-flavoured dish that usually lies very heavy on British stomachs.

Most savoys with firm heads are suitable for cabbage salad, and so are some cabbages that are not too coarse, particularly that excellent Alsatian variety, Quintal d'Alsace, which the late E. A. Bunyard did so much to popularise in the British Isles. After the outside leaves have been removed, the heart is finely shredded with a sharp knife. A tablespoonful of tarragon vinegar and four tablespoonfuls of salad oil with the necessary pepper and salt are needed for the shredded heart of a large cabbage or savoy. The amount of dressing is more generous than for a summer salad and it should be added some time before serving so that the salad is well soaked in the dressing.—E. H. M. COX

FEBRUARY 27TH, 1942

UNCOMMON VEGETABLES TO ADD TO THE SEED ORDER

It is sometimes strange to think of the time when such exotic vegetables as Brussels chicory, celeriac and kohlrabi were not part of our diets, but here the writer encourages their use, while also damning the prize-winning marrows for a lack of flavour.

I T IS NO less necessary to exercise initiative and enterprise in the choice and growing of vegetables than it is in the invention and production of vital accessories to the military effort. It is astonishing how so many people take such little interest in vegetables until they arrive at the table, and if the war has done any good at all so far, it is that it has taught gardeners to use a little more care in ordering their vegetables and has enabled many to make the acquaintance of several kinds hitherto entirely unknown.

"CALABRESE IS ONE OF THE ARISTOCRATS OF THE BRASSICA TRIBE"

Let us start with beans. The last years have for the first time brought home to many the virtues of the haricot bean, among which there is none better than the brown-seeded Dutch, now fortunately more plentiful than it was, and the white-seeded Comtesse de Chambord.

The unfortunate habit of judges in awarding prizes only to those vegetable marrows of the most enormous bulk has done much to discredit this vegetable in the eyes of the gourmet. The best marrows are undoubtedly White Custard, and those with custard blood in them like Table Dainty. And Rotherside Orange is, to my mind, the best of all, with fruits about half as large again as a grapefruit and with orange-coloured flesh.

Chicory is so easy to grow and makes one of the best winter salads.

The Witloof or Brussels chicory is the best for forming a solid heart and tastes almost as good raw as when cooked.

Those who do not know the turnip-rooted form of celery – celeriac – will find it worth a trial. The venturesome might also try kohlrabi, sometimes referred to as the turnip-rooted cabbage because of its flavour, which is reminiscent of each.

Calabrese, a green sprouting broccoli, is one of the aristocrats of the brassica tribe.

It is fairly safe to prophesy that cucumbers will be scarce this year, and gardeners will find a sowing of ridge or apple cucumber well worthwhile. Despite their ungainly shapes, the ridge cucumbers make excellent eating if gathered before they pass their youth.

In concluding this brief list, I specially mention the Welsh onion and the tree onion – both useful war-time crops. And yellow tomatoes are simply not grown as much as they should be. Yellow varieties like Golden Sunrise or Golden Nugget will appeal to every epicure, as will the pinkish-fruited variety called Peach Blow.—G. C. T.

FLOWER & FRUIT FARMS OF GREAT BRITAIN

Vegetables And . . . . Flowers . . From Seed.

ON PLANTING AN ORCHARD

By Marjory Allen

A confident, stentorian tone is characteristic of much writing in the early years of Country Life. *Here Marjory Allen offers practical advice on how to plant an orchard.*

THERE ARE FOUR main shapes of trees on the market:

Standards: slow in bearing but have long lives and large crops. Plant 25–30 ft. apart.

Half Standards: form large trees which produce heavy and good quality crops. Plant 20–30 ft. apart.

Bush trees: need careful cultivation but produce fine dessert apples and pears. Plant 12–18 ft. apart.

Espaliers and Cordons: produce fruit of the highest quality – apples and pears are usually grown in this way. Espaliers consist of a main stem with two, four, six or eight lateral branches trained horizontally to wires or strong wooden latticework. Cordons consist of one main stem with no lateral branches, and the fruit is produced from spurs arising from it. Leave 2 ft. 6 in. between the trees and plant in rows 6 ft. apart.

꿍

Plant in any of the following ways, using the measurements already given:

Square (See Fig. 1).—The land is marked out in a series of squares. The Quincunx system is similar to this, except that a permanent tree, of compact upright habit, is planted in the centre of each square.

Triangular—The trees are planted alternately in rows, equidistant at all points. It is difficult to thin the trees under this method, but undercropping is just as conveniently arranged.

When it comes to marking out your orchard, do not use twine or rope as a measurement guide as it is liable to stretch and throw the lines out of true; a surveyor's chain is usually easy to borrow.

ᠥᠥᠥ

Square or Quincunx (Fig. 1).—Decide on the base line of the plot and mark out the positions of the trees with stakes. Then set off two lines at right angles to it at its extreme ends. Connect E and F with the chain and mark off the position of each tree on that line also. Continue until the plot is complete.

Triangular (Fig. 2).—Mark off the base line KD and the two extreme lines at right angles, as for the square planting, then mark off the tree positions on the two side lines. Mark off at an angle of 30° from the end of the base line, a line KL, and mark NM running parallel to it. Mark off the trees at the distance required on these two lines and continue until the plot is covered.

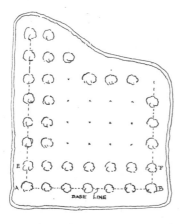

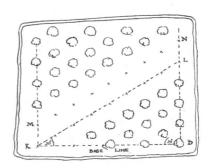

Fig. 1   Fig. 2

AUGUST 17TH, 1940

THE GIANT GOOSEBERRY BUSINESS

To the Editor of "Country Life."

Sir,—It is gratifying to note that in spite of the war some of the old Berry Societies are holding their annual Show, as they have done for scores and scores of years. There was one last week at Egton Bridge, near Whitby, and although the weather has not been as the growers would like, there were still some fine gooseberries on the stages. Among the real Yorkshire growers this art has been cultivated to an amazing degree: short stunted bushes not 2 ft. high are watered, mulched and tended like children till the fruit appears. Then the last week or so before a Show, small nets support the possible winners. When a real champion arrives – and the expert has a very shrewd idea long before it is ripe – then it has been known to be watched or guarded day and night till the crucial moment arrives for picking. It is amazing what a size these gooseberries will attain when properly looked after and, of course, a burst through over-ripeness before the show is just a terrible disaster. The size is almost unbelievable, but it is the weight that wins silver cups. A champion may weigh anything from 24 dwt to 28 dwt, and a silver challenge cup was taken last year with a Grand White just tipping the scale at 27 dwt, 8 grains. The unbeaten champion, produced many years ago, was a Red Bobby, weighing 30 dwt, 15 grains.—H. C. BUCKLE

> "IN SPITE OF THE WAR SOME OF THE OLD BERRY SOCIETIES ARE HOLDING THEIR ANNUAL SHOW"

"A burst through over-ripeness before the show is just a
terrible disaster."

MARCH 3ᴿᴰ, 1917

CROPPING A 10 ROD ALLOTMENT

There was an obsession with digging up lawns to plant potatoes during World War I, and when the seed potatoes became scarce, Country Life *was able to suggest alternatives.*

IN CROPPING AN allotment this year, allowances have to be made for some very unusual and disturbing circumstances. In the first place, the shortage of seed potatoes is certain to throw many an allotment holder out of his reckoning. To allow for this, additional space should be given to Jerusalem artichokes and parsnips, both of which are excellent substitutes and may be expected to give good returns in newly broken land. Then we have to replace the spring cabbages, lettuces and winter greens that have been destroyed by the exceptionally severe weather. To do this it is advisable to sow at once such quick-growing cabbages as Sutton's Earliest, Flower of Spring, and Harbinger. These should be sown under glass, and this is where a garden frame will come in very useful. The young cabbage heads may not be so firm and tightly packed as those which stand the winter, but when cooked they will prove more tender, milder in flavour, and of better colour. The quicker a cabbage is grown, the better it is on the table.

> "THE SHORTAGE OF SEED POTATOES IS CERTAIN TO THROW MANY AN ALLOTMENT HOLDER OUT OF HIS RECKONING"

CROPPING A 10 ROD ALLOTMENT.

JERUSALEM ARTICHOKES. *Rows two feet apart.* *Plant tubers now.*	6ft.

RHUBARB.	*Seed bed for raising young vegetables.*	*Frame.*	4ft.

BROAD BEANS.
Two rows. Sow now. Brussels Sprouts to follow.
4ft.

EARLY POTATOES.
Four rows 2ft. 6in. apart. Plant sprouted sets late March. Plant Winter Greens between rows in June.

LATE POTATOES.
Four rows 2ft. 6in. apart. Plant in late March Lift in October and sow Turnips.

20ft.

PARSNIPS.
Six rows. Sow now.
8ft.

CARROTS.
Four rows. Sow March and April.
4ft.

ONIONS.
Eight rows. Four rows sow March and April. Two rows transplanted winter varieties. Two rows plant sets now.
8ft.

SPRING CABBAGES.
Two rows, 2ft. apart. Sow at once in frames. Dwarf French Beans to follow.

EARLY LETTUCE.
Three rows. Sow now. Perpetual Spinach and Tomatoes to follow.
8ft.

DWARF PEAS.
Two rows. Sow now. Plant Celery between rows a few weeks before Peas are gathered.
4ft.

SHALLOTS.
Four rows. Plant now. Shorthorn Carrots and Lettuce to follow.
4ft.

BEETROOT.
One row Globe, sow late March. Two rows Long, sow May.
4ft.

TURNIPS.
Four rows. Sow late March. Leeks to follow. Sow April; plant June.
6ft.

DWARF FRENCH BEANS. *Three rows. Sow in May.*	*Marrow Bed.*	5ft.

RUNNER BEANS. *One row. Sow in May.*	*Rubbish Heap.*	5ft. 9in.

90ft. 9in.

30ft.

65

THE EPICURE IN SEARCH
OF VEGETABLES

THE WISEST MODERN doctors tell us to eat good greenmeat more than we do, but where are we to get it? The late Sir Richard Owen used to tell me that man was a fruit- and shoot-eating animal by nature, though omnivorous as regards other things, especially when he had nothing else. As I write, there is an article in the *Lancet* on our indebtedness to the vegetable kingdom, so we are fortified by scientific opinion as to their value as a food.

The first thing to do is to have a general change of plan in gardens. People in towns must take what they can get, but country people grow too much the coarser vegetables, like cabbage and potatoes, in good garden ground, when these can be grown anywhere. A certain proportion of the ground should be given to other things, but the question for the present is what we can get now.

> **"TO SERVE SPINACH WELL IS THE MARK OF A GOOD COOK"**

Hard winters are those that test us most, and there should be more trials of green vegetables that endure a hard winter. A friend, writing to me from the Midlands, says: "In our garden we have not a bit of green stuff in the place – all is killed outright." I think it would be worth the while of our great seedsmen if, instead of endeavouring to surpass each other with the big bean or the big marrow, they would turn their attention to this very important subject of raising and experimenting with really hardy green vegetables.

An excellent vegetable has come in, mostly from abroad, and that is chicory – known to the Belgians as witloof. It is simply one of the strong forms of our common chicory which one sees in beautiful bloom in chalky fields sometimes. This comes in considerable quantities from abroad but really ought to be grown at home as it is a strong vegetable and easily blanched, even in the shed. Its bitter flavour is welcome and there is, happily, no difficulty about its cooking.

One vegetable which our climate is very kind to is spinach, but it is ill-treated by the cooks and so often overloaded with grease and spice that its flavour and good qualities are wholly destroyed. A French bishop, who was asked to dinner by a friend to test the quality of a new cook said, when questioned about his dinner, "I am waiting for the spinach." He was quite right: to serve it well is the mark of a good cook.

A common vegetable, and one I think is very much under-valued, is the Jerusalem artichoke. It is not really an artichoke, but a tuberous sunflower. It is despised because it is often served with a sort of paste – such as is used to paste on the placards – but if braised and served in other ways it is a very good and wholesome vegetable. It is a much more toothsome food than fried potatoes and it makes the nicest chips we know of to go with game.

OCTOBER 10TH, 1897

BRITISH FRUIT AT CRYSTAL PALACE

THE THREE DAYS' exhibition recently held under the auspices of the Royal Horticultural Society at the Crystal Palace was a revelation of the capabilities of our sea-girt isles in the production of high-class fruit. Rich produce and, perhaps, rosier apples come from sunnier lands, but for quality no imports can beat the specimens that our land supplies. Fruit growers have much to thank the Royal Horticultural Society for in awakening a keen interest in an important industry.

We do not despise the ruddy fruits from our colonies, rather rejoice in the produce our countrymen from over the seas export, but we must ever remember that the British Isles can give splendid results, too, if a reasonable number of varieties is grown, not a medley of indifferent kinds.

> "A REVELATION OF THE CAPABILITIES OF OUR SEA-GIRT ISLES"

The miscellaneous portion of the show was very beautiful. A centre of attraction was the noble group from Her Majesty's gardens at Frogmore. Apples, pears, and, indeed, fruits of many kinds composed this conspicuous trophy, the new golden Jubilee tomato, surrounded with pine-apples, forming a showy and bold feature. This new tomato was raised, we believe, by Mr. Owen Thomas, the Queen's gardener. Its colour is clear golden yellow, and the flavour is of great delicacy.

We were pleased to see such prominence given to a valuable fruit. Tomato growing has attained huge proportions during the Queen's reign; new and excellent varieties have been raised, and the fruit used in many ways. It is not unlikely that in the near future the smaller kinds of delicate flavour will form part of the choicest dessert. Many uses may be made of the tomato, some preferring raw fruit, others prepared in various dainty styles.

FEBRUARY 17TH, 1917

CONVERTING LAWNS AND PLEASURE GROUNDS INTO POTATO PLOTS

An intense debate was conducted in the editorial and correspondence pages of Country Life *on the best way to increase food production in times of war. Here a correspondent calls for a more restrained and sensible approach to producing potatoes.*

TO THE EDITOR OF "COUNTRY LIFE."

SIR,—It is not pleasant to risk being accused of trying to damp down such patriotic spirit, but the mere suggestion of the conversion of ordinary lawns or pleasure grounds into potato plots compels the thought that perhaps zeal is outrunning discretion. There are doubtless some extensive lawns and the like which could, perhaps advantageously, be made to yield crops, but are there not as many others in which the results could scarcely be looked forward to? So far as the coming season's crop is concerned, the all-important question must be that of labour and manure, and in most instances there are probably fields adjoining the lawns, or in the near vicinity, upon which these could be far more expeditiously and profitably employed. To divert either labour or manure from the fields to the lawn would surely be poor economy at the present time.—GEORGE BOLAM

"IT IS NOT PLEASANT TO RISK BEING ACCUSED OF TRYING TO DAMP DOWN SUCH PATRIOTIC SPIRIT"

JANUARY 28TH, 1905

THE USE OF SORREL

A CORRESPONDENT WRITES to ask whether Sorrel is much grown nowadays, and to this we must answer that it is as uncommon as Salsafy and Scorzonera – two excellent vegetables which the Frenchman appreciates, but the Englishman ignores. Sorrel is a wholesome salad and a good vegetable. There are few varieties of it, and the large-leaved ones are the most nutritious and agreeable, having little of that undesirable bitterness which makes the small-leaved forms obnoxious. We are constantly urging that a greater variety of vegetables should be introduced into the English garden and Sorrel would make a welcome change, either served alone or in the salad bowl. A well-known grower of vegetables writes: "Sorrel is greatly

> "EXCELLENT VEGETABLES WHICH THE FRENCHMAN APPRECIATES, BUT THE ENGLISHMAN IGNORES"

improved by culture, as the leaves then become more solid and therefore more useful. The common Sorrel is a native of Great Britain, running riot in swampy pastures. In dry soil it runs to seed. I do not recommend the British plant for garden cultivation, but rather the Continental variety of French Sorrel, known as the Belleville. This has large leaves, sweeter than those of the common kind, and when the plant is well grown it is a delicious vegetable. It is grown largely for the Paris markets, and has a great sale. The plant is easily raised from seed, or by dividing the roots in early March. Leaves suitable for salad can be obtained in two or three months."

JULY 6ᵀᴴ, 1918

OUR VEGETABLE GARDEN

BY GEN. THE HON. SIR JULIAN BYNG, K.C.B., K.C.M.G.

A correspondent's remarkable efforts to tame a wilderness succeed, producing an impressive quantity and variety of vegetables during a hungry period.

SINCE NOWADAYS FLOWER-GARDENING no longer exists, and we all turn our energies to the production of food, I thought it might interest your readers to see this photograph, taken on June 1st, of a soldier's garden during his absence on service in France. We came to this house in 1914 to find a wilderness forested with nettles and thistles against which we still wage ceaseless war, and it has been no easy task to turn desolation into food. In 1917 I decided to crop every corner of the place for our own use and that of local troops and, thanks to the untiring efforts of our excellent gardener R. Moore, we have been fairly successful.

> "WE FOUND A WILDERNESS FORESTED WITH NETTLES AGAINST WHICH WE STILL WAGE CEASELESS WAR"

We have plenty of Cuthbert's Giant White Cos lettuces, and a newly planted orchard with ground cropped with cabbages, carrots, beet, beans, shallots, Chinese artichokes, seakale and peas. A pear wall facing east has potato May Queen in the foreground, and between the fruit trees Cuthbert's Open-Air tomato, with Dutch brown beans as an edging.

Since dried fruit for cakes is *non est*, we have planted a good-sized patch of caraway seed, and on ground that is neither sufficiently good nor cleaned for vegetables, we have grown sunflowers for chicken food. In the borders near the house are broad beans with a big edging of curled parsley.

Our inside space consists of two small three-quarter span houses and a little double span greenhouse purchased from the postmaster, and here we have an abundant promise of good things beloved of the soldier. Besides the tomatoes – our pride and joy – ridge cucumbers are another delicacy much liked by the troops, and the backyard rejoices in these.

We have in all about four and three-quarter acres thus cropped with vegetables, including potatoes, and the varieties of the latter are Evergood, King Edward, Beauty of Hebron, and Ninetyfold.

"A Great Kale" Jan 2ND, 1937

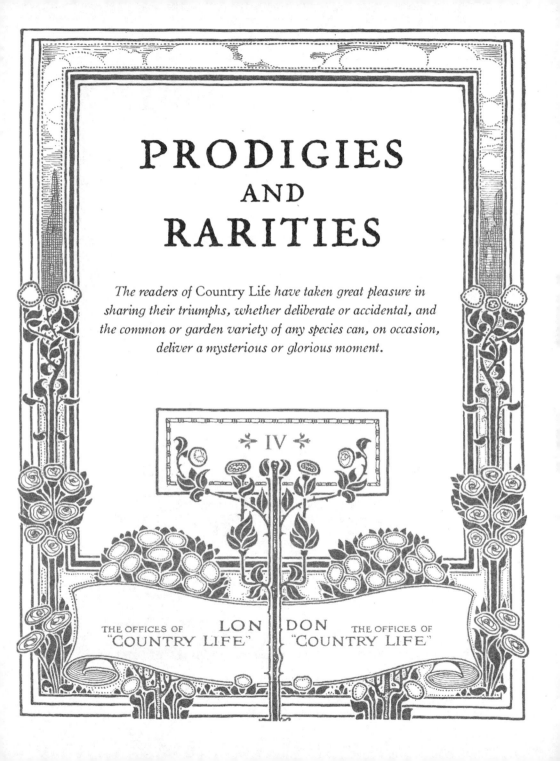

PRODIGIES
AND
RARITIES

The readers of Country Life *have taken great pleasure in sharing their triumphs, whether deliberate or accidental, and the common or garden variety of any species can, on occasion, deliver a mysterious or glorious moment.*

✦ IV ✦

LONDON

THE OFFICES OF "COUNTRY LIFE"

THE OFFICES OF "COUNTRY LIFE"

MARCH 1ST, 1930

A LIVE LATTICEWORK

TO THE EDITOR OF "COUNTRY LIFE."

SIR,—The enclosed photograph of a hornbeam hedge may interest your readers. This hedge forms the boundary fence of the Presbytery garden at Tessé-la-Madelaine, Bagnoles-de-l'Orne, France. As will be seen, the garden is raised above the road by about 3 ft. 6 in., and kept up by a grass bank. The latticework over this bank is live hornbeam, kept clear of leaves. In some places the hornbeam, at the intersection of the lattice, has made a complete graft. In the upper part the hedge is kept trimmed in the form shown in the photograph. It is curious that the hedge should grow as well as it has done, for the grass bank is nearly upright and almost on the same face as the hedge above it. Inside the hedge is a path under which the roots of the hornbeam must find their nourishment. There is a similar hedge at the railway station of Briouze, not far from Bagnoles, but there the lower part is not kept clear of leaves and is left to form a closely trimmed hedge.—A. A. HUDSON

JULY 5ᵀᴴ, 1930

A GIANT RUBBER TREE

To the Editor of "Country Life."

Sir,—The *Ficus elastica* is only one species of the gum genus, which produce caoutchouc, labelled "rubber". *Ficus elastica* grows very rapidly, but when mature they do not bleed or give latex (milk) in the same manner as does the *Hevea brasiliensis*. The method of getting the caoutchouc from the Ficus was to climb the tree and hack it with a hatchet or parang, to let it bleed, and then to collect the coagulum from the surface of the limb of the tree. But the amount of coagulum so produced was not commensurate with the labour involved and compared unfavourably with *Hevea* species.

> "IN OUR IGNORANCE, WE BLED THE TREE WITH EIGHT WICKED CUTS DAILY"

We used to tap the *Hevea* on the herring-bone system, about eight or ten wicked cuts leading to a channel which led to the collecting cup. But we have learnt wisdom as regards "bark reserves", and we now only make one cut, about a half or third of the circumference of the stem, and only on alternate days: year in and year out we now get more dry rubber per tree per annum than we did when, in our ignorance, we bled the tree with eight wicked cuts daily.—J. S. M. Rennie

AUGUST 8TH, 1931

TAILS INSTEAD OF HEADS: A PERVERSE HOLLYHOCK

To the Editor of "Country Life."

SIR,—You may, perhaps, be interested in this photograph of a freak hollyhock, now blooming in the garden of Mr. Denman of Crown Street, Darlington. As you will see, the bloom is at the bottom instead of at the top. This is surely unique, is it not?—W. T. Broumley

[The picture is certainly that of a very interesting eccentricity. We have never in our experience seen or heard of a hollyhock blooming in this way.—Ed]

NOVEMBER 28TH, 1931

HOW DID THE APPLE GET INSIDE THE DUMPLING?

To the Editor of "Country Life."

Sir,—This apple was picked off a Blenheim apple tree on the premises of an old forge at Hendon, N.W. London, inhabited by the family of Suckling for over a hundred years. An old tennis ball, partly chewed by their dog, was thrown away, and it lodged on the apple tree during this year and remained there until the apples were picked. The ball must have fallen on one of the blossoms as, much to the surprise of the family, one of the apples had grown inside it, as the photograph clearly shows.—
Edgar Loewenthal

AUGUST 18TH, 1934

WALKING ON A HEDGE

To the Editor of "Country Life."

Sir,—I send you a photograph which will, I think, be of interest. The men are at Powis Castle clipping the yew hedge, the top of which is so firm from constant clipping that you can see the Head Gardener walking about on the top of the hedge. The hedge is about 45 ft. high and is over 200 years old.—Powis

OCTOBER 5ᵀᴴ, 1901

LILIUM AURATUM PLATYPHYLLUM

TO THE EDITOR OF "COUNTRY LIFE."

SIR,—I send you a photograph of a bed of *Lilium auratum* (*platyphyllum*) in this garden, as they are generally considered to be very fine and it may interest the readers of COUNTRY LIFE to know how they are grown so successfully. I imported the bulbs four years ago and they were planted in the peat of a rhododendron bed with a little leaf mould added. Nothing more has been done to them since except that during the winter they are covered over with a few ashes. From the first they have done very well, and have improved every year both in strength and number. Many of them have this year had between thirty and forty blooms, all large and well marked; the tallest was 8 ft. 6 in. high, and several others were nearly as tall. No manure has ever been put to them, and the secret seems to be planting them deep, about 16 in., in peat and in the shade of a rhododendron. Though it is very dry here, no water was given at any time during the summer.—COBHAM C. KNIGHT

A DREAM OF PUMPKINS

TO THE EDITOR OF "COUNTRY LIFE."

SIR,—I am sending you a photograph of the champion pumpkin which I grew at Hembury House, Radlett, last year. It measured 7 ft. 3 in. in circumference and weighed 136 lb. The prize it won and the sum for which it was sold to a London store were divided between local charities and, in addition, its seeds were sold for the benefit of a children's hospital. It made £15 alone in the prize and price realised, in addition to which its flesh was sold at sixpence per pound for making delicious pumpkin jam and pies. You will notice it produced 334 seeds, and one client alone purchased one hundred seeds at sixpence each.

> **"IT MEASURED 7 FT. 3 IN. IN CIRCUMFERENCE AND WEIGHED 136 LB."**

If each of the seeds produces a similar pumpkin, the total weight will be 20 tons, 5 cwt, and at sixpence per pound this would realise £1,134.

334 pumpkins selling at £10 each would realise £3,340.

334 first prizes at £5 each (if there were enough competitions) would realise £1,670.

111,556 seeds at sixpence each would realise £2,788 18s.

Grand total: £8,932 18s

—H. Y. NUTT

OCTOBER 12TH, 1901

A CURIOUS APPLE FREAK

To THE EDITOR OF "COUNTRY LIFE."

SIR,—I beg to enclose a photograph of a stem of an apple tree in my orchard. From the centre of the stem, where there is no branch, you will observe a bunch of five apples which have grown out from the main stem of the tree. My gardener observed a few blossoms from a little bud sticking out of the bark, from whence the apples have matured. Should you think the circumstance sufficiently interesting, you are welcome to put the photograph in one of your issues.—D. M. CRICHTON MAITLAND (MAJOR-GENERAL)

[It is certainly interesting. It is evidently the result of a little flowering shoot from the stem of the tree, and should not be regarded as a "freak," as the cluster is the outcome of perfect flowers, and bunches or clusters like this are not uncommon among apples.—Ed]

FEBRUARY 20TH, 1932

"TILL BIRNAM WOOD DO COME TO DUNSINANE"

Not, perhaps, the most economical manner of blocking a development of new flats from view, but certainly an effective solution. The sentiment will strike a chord with many readers of Country Life *today.*

To the Editor of "Country Life."

Sir,—You may care to see this photograph showing how a whole group of trees were transplanted in the grounds of a house at Campden Hill. The task was undertaken because the owner of the house wanted to shut out the view of a block of flats near at hand. One of the trees is 70 ft. high and weighs over 30 tons.—H.

DECEMBER 10TH, 1921

THE YUCCA

To the Editor of "Country Life."

SIR,—In a recent edition you had an illustration showing, among other plants, the *Yucca filamentosa* in the garden at Sedgwick Park, Horsham. The enclosed photograph may, therefore, be of sufficient interest for you to publish. I believe it is quite unusual to have so many blooms – there were thirty-two all told – and the Director of the Botanic Gardens at Kew tells me it is exceptional in this country. The plants have flowered the last two years, but only two or three blooms. How long they have been planted in these gardens here I do not know, as I have only been in possession of this house (at Bristol) for the last three years.—HORACE WALKER

"THEY ARE NEVER SEEN SO EFFECTIVELY AS UNDER THE LIGHT OF THE MOON"

[The group is unusually well flowered, but yuccas have blossomed extraordinarily well this season. The plants illustrated, though fine, do not represent the best type of Yucca gloriosa. *The finest form of this plant has narrower leaves, a more pyramidal spike and, when old, a more tree-like habit. This latter type cannot, unfortunately, be relied upon to succeed in the Midlands or North of England. Our correspondent's bed is of a type of plant reminiscent in habit of the more commonly seen* Yucca recurvifolia. *This, too, is an excellent plant, but the brown backs to the sepals detract to some extent from its effect when in flower. As one would expect from their colouration, yuccas depend on night-flying insects for their fertilisation. Their flowers, therefore, open wider by night, so that they are never seen so effectively as under the light of the moon, which always deals kindly with flowers of cream or greenish colouring.—Ed]*

MARCH 13TH, 1905

THE PEAR TREE AT DEAL CASTLE

IN THE MOAT encircling the Round Tower of Windsor there was once a vineyard, and the moat at Buckling in Norfolk now grows flowers in place of fish. But the idea of converting the dry ditch of the stout old fortress at Deal Castle, built by Henry VIII on the very margin of the sea, into a siege garden capable of supplying the governors with dessert in summer and with unlimited supplies of stewed fruit in winter, will strike most people as no less ingenious than original.

The fortress itself consists of an elaborate series of half-moon harbours and a large central circular tower. A deep ditch, very broad and with a masonry wall on the outer side, runs around the whole structure. Though the structure is in perfect repair, nearly four centuries of time have covered the stones with flowering plants and ivy in places, and convened the whole of the flat bottom of the ditch into a smooth green lawn.

"BUT HIS LORDSHIP HAD A GARDENER, A MAN OF ORIGINALITY AND SENSE"

A century ago, Lord Carrington had Deal Castle as his residence, and this Lord Carrington at once adorned and disfigured the castle. On one of its sea-facing bastions he constructed a "Carpenter's Gothic" erection of brick and stucco, painted a cheerful lead colour so ugly and so screamingly at variance with the solid sense and congruity of the rest of the structure that it has evoked the irrepressible censure of everyone who has since looked upon it.

But his lordship had a gardener, a man of originality and sense, and Mr. Ricketts – for that was his name – soon saw that the moat of the castle was the only part of the demesne on which any thing but seaweed would grow. There now grows an exquisitely trained pear tree, planted by Mr. Ricketts, which is lovely at any time but particularly beautiful at this season when the clumps of blossom are set off by the grey stones below. The pear tree is accompanied by figs, and the effect is quite remarkable.—C. J. CORNISH

APRIL 29TH, 1911

A TINY GREENHOUSE

To the Editor of "Country Life."

SIR,—About six years ago the matron of the hospital here gave the porter some empty urine bottles which had been in a bottle-rack in the yard of the hospital. The porter made an edging to his garden path by burying the bottles with their necks downwards in the gravel so that about half the bottle was out of the ground. A few days ago he was surprised to see that something was growing in the bottles and he pulled some up. I am sending you two of the bottles. There are indoor ferns in them all, with their roots in the necks of the bottles. One is the ribbon fern and I do not know the name of the other, but recognised it as a fern one often sees in pots in rooms and greenhouses.—J. E. BULLAN

[The ferns referred to by our correspondent are Pteris cretica, *which is illustrated, and* Pteris tremula, *both of which require greenhouse or similar protection in this country. We have seen and heard of several instances where hardy ferns have grown in bottles in this way, but do not remember an instance of greenhouse ferns flourishing outdoors with only the protection of an ordinary glass bottle. The two plants have no doubt originated from the spores which are produced freely by these species. These spores might have found their way to the garden path via sweepings or dustings from a room in which the parent plants were growing. The longevity of fern spores is known to be very great, and the circumstances under which they will germinate are evidently widely varied.—Ed]*

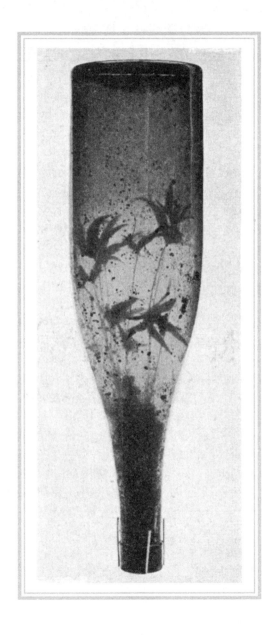

THE INTELLIGENCE OF VEGETABLE MARROWS

Infectious enthusiasm, curiosity and generosity are hallmarks of much of the correspondence from Country Life's *gardeners.*

TO THE EDITOR OF "COUNTRY LIFE."

SIR,—Perhaps few people would give vegetable marrows credit for intelligence. Their name is against them and usually they occupy a very humble corner of the kitchen garden. I have been watching one at Yarne, near Cobham, with great interest. It had one strong stem 15 ft. long before I noticed it and this grew horizontally along the south-east side of the garden and only about 7 in. below the top of a thick-clipped box hedge which stands at 4 ft. high.

Last Sunday we planted two strong pea sticks on the north-west side of the hedge, not touching it, and on Monday morning the marrow had put out two arms which had grown up and over the hedge and taken a firm hold of both pea sticks. I then put two stakes, one firmly fixed and the other loosely standing, on the north-west side of the hedge but some way from the pea sticks. A few hours later two more arms appeared over the hedge and one gripped the firm stake tightly; the other apparently tested the loose stake and, finding it shaky and unsafe, passed it by and instead took hold of the nearby hedge. We then planted a strong pea stick a few inches from the very end of the marrow's 15 ft. stem and, of course, on the opposite side of the hedge. The marrow, obviously pleased, raised its head at almost a right angle to its body and today, Wednesday, it is making a bee-line for the pea stick. If this is not intelligence, what is it? Perhaps some of your readers will watch their marrow plants before the growing season is over and report anything of interest.—ELLINOR C. L. CLOSE

DECEMBER 31ST, 1938
THE INSANE ROOT

To the Editor of "Country Life."

SIR,—I am sure you must be inundated with pictures every autumn of curious roots, but even so I cannot forbear to send you this photograph of a potato sprouting.

I do hope you will be able to include it in your Correspondence columns, for I feel that it is too good to be missed.

It seems to need no explanation, but I would point out that the face seems to me to have a beautiful expression.

It is perfectly astonishing that it should have grown two ears and a tail.—TREVOR LEIGHTON

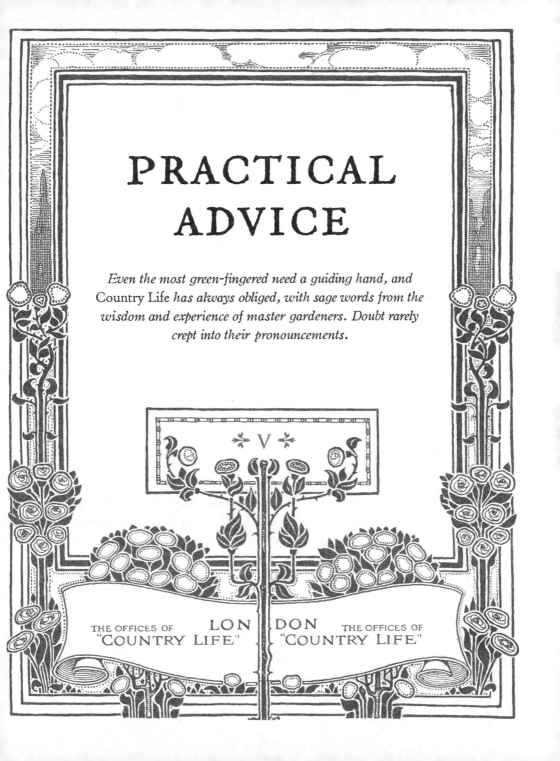

PRACTICAL
ADVICE

Even the most green-fingered need a guiding hand, and
Country Life *has always obliged, with sage words from the*
wisdom and experience of master gardeners. Doubt rarely
crept into their pronouncements.

V

THE OFFICES OF   LON   DON   THE OFFICES OF
"COUNTRY LIFE"   "COUNTRY LIFE"

WINTER WORK IN THE FRUIT GARDEN

Timely advice at the start of the winter for those with orchards.

THE PROGRAMME OF winter work in the orchard and fruit garden is not altogether a light one. Nor can there be delay in carrying out the work, as unkindly weather conditions will almost certainly hold up operations for long spells at a time.

It is important to carry out the necessary duties in sequence: spraying should follow and not precede pruning, followed again by ground cultivation. The best time to prune orchard trees is as soon as their leaves have fallen, and there is no better time than the present for the work.

> "THERE IS NO BETTER TIME THAN THE PRESENT"

The pruner is chiefly concerned with shaping the trees and the removal of growths – apple and pear scab, canker, mildew, brown rot and like diseases all pass the winter in the wood of affected growths. Spraying cannot cure these prevalent ailments, and diseased wood remains a centre of infection each spring.

Another duty of the pruner is to "thin out" crowded branches and growths. When the head of the tree is choked with tangled growths, fruitfulness is seriously impaired and disease directly encouraged; the centres of the trees and bushes should be kept open and free from crossing growths so that sunlight is admitted to every part at all times of the year and air can circulate freely.

If there is occasion to use the pruning saw, it is of the utmost importance to smooth the jagged edges of the saw-cut and to cover the entire cut surface with a generous coating of white lead paint or Stockholm tar to keep out disease.

SEPTEMBER 12TH, 1925

THE COST OF OUR FLOWERS

After World War I many private households could no longer afford staff, nor to garden on the scale previously enjoyed.

I T IS A bother when working on a hobby to have to think of money, money, money; but gardening, however hard you may work at it, is always a hobby and a pleasant recreation – but still it costs money. There is little doubt that, before the war, many glorious gardens were run on extravagant lines; but then labour and coal – always the most expensive part of a garden – were cheaper than in these post-war days. This change, however, from pre-war to post-war conditions has left many

owners of gardens at a loss what to do. There may have been little need for economy in the old days, and certainly in many gardens none was practised. Now that economy is the order of the day, they do not know where to begin, except by the obvious means of reducing labour costs and closing down glasshouses and, perhaps, allowing a portion of their garden to run to rack and ruin.

"THE VOGUE OF THE WILD GARDEN"

The necessity for economy in gardening is teaching us two great lessons – the economy that is made by the more extensive use of shrubs and the vogue of the wild garden, which is so inexpensive to run. —E. H. M. Cox

DECEMBER 10TH, 1904

A CURE FOR IVY POISONING

To the Editor of "Country Life."

Sir,—I notice in your paper an occasional reference to the annoyance of ivy poisoning, and it may be of use to know that a thick poultice of powdered cinnamon, mixed with water and applied to the parts affected, is regarded in this locality – among the mountains – as a quick and sure cure.—T. H. Bartlett, Chocorua, New Hampshire, U.S.A.

JANUARY 5TH, 1924

SPUR PRUNING OF APPLES AND PEARS

By E. A. Bunyard

To so many pruners, pruning means cutting back the long side shoots of last season's growth, and the spur, once formed, is given a grateful glance and passed over. But we have now come to a stage in which severe spur pruning is necessary for many reasons.

Firstly, it is physically impossible for each bud, even if it set only one fruit out of its five flowers, to carry the fruits in its limited space. If we imagine each fruit the size of a tennis ball, this becomes obvious.

"SEVERE SPUR PRUNING IS NECESSARY FOR MANY REASONS"

Secondly, the tree cannot support and nourish so many buds and their resulting fruits. For the food reserve in the tree is like money placed in a bank and, as we know only too well, we cannot withdraw from a bank more than we deposit. If fifty buds are drawing on the balance, it is obvious that their share will be less than if only ten buds were concerned, and this difference may be critical in leading a bud from the barren into the fruiting stage. How frequently we hear of trees which flower well but produce little fruit – old espaliers and wall trees being notorious offenders. Paradoxically enough, a reduction of fruit-buds may lead to an increase of fruit.

THIRD YEAR.

FOURTH YEAR.

SIXTH YEAR.

APRIL 17TH, 1937

A COUNTRYWOMAN'S REMEDY FOR "DOLPHIN"

To the Editor of "Country Life."

Sir,—Last year I was complaining sadly of the ravages of "dolphin" (the local name for black fly), when the woman who does my work told me that the water in which rhubarb leaves have been boiled would, if syringed over the broad beans, at once drive away the menace. My broad beans were very bad and I really had no faith in the supposed remedy, but I tried it. The first spraying certainly improved the beans, so the next day I syringed the beans again, and this time completely destroyed the black fly. I believe, however, that it would be most effective if the broad beans were sprayed when the blossoms first began to open. The oldest and coarsest rhubarb leaves should be used, roughly torn into shreds, and a couple of liberal handfuls placed in a large pan with a gallon and a half of water. Boil for ten minutes, allow to get cold, strain through a fine-mesh sieve, and use in the evening. A fine sieve is important, as otherwise the particles of boiled leaf are troublesome in the syringe. I have also found the rhubarb liquid a useful repellent of green fly on roses.—Phillipa Francklyn

"THE OLDEST AND COARSEST RHUBARB LEAVES SHOULD BE USED"

FEBRUARY 18TH, 1922

ON YEW HEDGES

By G. H. KITCHIN

SHAPING ANIMALS OUT of yew hedges is indeed difficult – it comes naturally to some people, but not everybody has the initiative and instinct necessary. For quick results it is of course possible to buy wire cages shaped like peacocks, weathercocks and foxes, which can be fixed to the top of the chosen bushes and into which all available boughs are crammed. The cages are soon hidden in greenery and will rust and disappear over time.

"THE MORE ABSURD THE BETTER"

But the results of this get-rich-quick method are really not as good as the genuine article. It is best not to be in too great a hurry, but to choose a strong central yew stem and let it grow more or less as it wants for two or three years until it shows a natural bias as to head, tail and general shape. With some bending, wiring and a little trimming, a beast of some sort can soon be

modelled – the more absurd the better – and its shape can be altered and improved upon as time goes by.

After yew, boxwood is the next best thing for topiary work, but it is more upright in growth and does not lend itself quite as well to the spreading tails of peacocks (even a yew peacock will sometimes have to have a brick tied to its tail for a year or two to keep it down, in spite of its more horizontal habit of growth).

When fastening boughs together or tying them in, pieces of hard wood should be inserted in the loop so as to take the cut of the wire and prevent it growing into the bark, thereby stopping the circulation. Sometimes a bough will absorb the ring of wire without any ill effects, but other times it will die, and it is best to be on the safe side.

Most people leave the work to their gardeners, but when you have mastered the use of the double-handled shears, it is a fascinating pursuit of a summer's evening, and one that grows in interest. There are infinite possibilities of improving outlines and of forming archways and objects, and there is always the satisfaction of going forth the next morning to admire, or otherwise, the fruits of your labours.

APRIL 1ST, 1899

SEASIDE SHELL GRAVEL FOR GARDEN PATHS

The Editor of Country Life *suggests some alternatives to gravel paths, or, should the correspondent still insist upon gravel, where it might be obtained.*

TO THE EDITOR OF "COUNTRY LIFE."

SIR,—I am anxious to procure some good seaside shell gravel for my garden paths. Could you, through the medium of your paper, inform me where I am likely to be able to get it?—WOODS

[You would be wise to obtain the seaside gravel, really shingle, from the mouth of the Severn, say Newport or Cardiff, as those places seem to be nearest to you by rail. But can you not obtain somewhere inland a better gravel than loose seaside shingle? It may be excellent material for making concrete walks – especially useful in such hilly districts as Malvern, where the heavy rains often upset gravel paths – but constantly walking upon a loose gravel path is a trial, not to mention the perpetual weed growth. We advise you to apply to the station agent at Malvern Links for information as to the cost of procuring gravel by rail, as cartage from there to you would be a considerable item. You would also do well to consult a local horticulturalist – perhaps one Mr. Fielder, the gardener at St. James's House. In these gardens, turf forms delightful walks and, when properly constructed, no walks can be better in a hilly district especially if, as in your case, gravel is difficult to obtain.—Ed]

APRIL IST, 1916

GRAFTING A STANDARD APPLE TREE

OR YEARS I HAD been dissatisfied with my apple tree. It was an unnamed variety and a poor cropper – in short, it was not worth the space it occupied. It would have been a great pity to destroy the tree for, despite its faults, it made a shapely and healthy looking standard. It was therefore decided to cut back the stock's branches and to graft a new head to the old shoulders.

The work was taken in hand in the spring of 1903 and the variety selected was Cox's Orange Pippin – an excellent apple that is known to do well in the district. A few weeks before the grafting, the main branches of the stock were sawn off to within 2 ft. of the main stem. The scions of Pippin were about as thick as a pencil, and 6 or 8 in. long when prepared.

> "FOR YEARS
> I HAD BEEN
> DISSATISFIED
> WITH MY
> APPLE TREE"

Just before grafting, a few more inches were sawn off each branch of the stock tree, and the wood pared off smoothly.

There are several ways of grafting standards, but the method applied in this case was that known as crown or rind grafting. That is, to insert the scions just within the bark of the tree. In preparing the scions, the bottom 2 or 3 in. of each was pared off in a slanting direction – a practised hand can do this in one clean cut. The bark of the stock was easily raised with the haft of a budding knife, and the scion – or even two or three – was pushed into position. The whole was then bound with broad strands of raffia.

It is important that the work be carried out speedily and, once completed, either grafting wax or clay must be used to prevent air, rain or frost from reaching the place of union.

In due season, every graft showed signs of growth and some have since been thinned out to prevent overcrowding. A new head was formed on the shoulders of the old tree before the summer of 1913 was over, and a little pruning has since enabled the tree to produce an ample supply of fruiting wood.—H. C.

IN THE GARDEN

TREE CUT BACK AND GRAFTS INSERTED.

GRAFTS COATED WITH CLAY.

THE FIRST YEAR'S GROWTH.

AUGUST 15TH, 1925

A GARDENING NOTEBOOK

As E. H. M. Cox makes very clear, no serious gardener should ever be caught without his or her notebook.

NOTEBOOK IS of incalculable service to every conscientious gardener, and the compiling of a gardening notebook should be a labour of love. It should state successes and failures frankly, shortly, and to the point.

This is the time of year during which such a notebook should be started, for there is a pause in work in the garden, most plants are at their maximum of development, and the results of the labours of autumn, winter and spring are enjoyed.

Here are a few of the points which might be noted:

"A GARDENING NOTEBOOK SHOULD BE A LABOUR OF LOVE"

As regards the herbaceous border: note down if the colour scheme is unsuitable, which plants to move, which to throw away, and so on. Make a careful note of any particularly vigorous plant so that this may be propagated or divided in due season. It is almost impossible to remember the exact size, shape and colour of plants when the growth has disappeared, so note now any bare patches or poor corners. And list any favourable plants noticed in other gardens so that they may be obtained, either by purchase or exchange, before next season.

These are a few of the points that come to mind; there are of course dozens more which could be noted.—E. H. M. COX

JUNE 21ST, 1941

HOW TO MAKE COWSLIP BALLS

Sir,—Miss Delafield lamented in your Summer Number the fact that few people now know how to make cowslip balls. This seems so very strange and sad to me that I really am sorry for them and hasten to give the recipe, though I fear that my letter may be too late to lead to any great output of cowslip balls this season.

My mother used to bring a big bunch of cowslips into our nursery and we were allowed, if old enough to understand, to break off the stems close to each head of flowers. Then two chairs were put back to back with perhaps a yard's space between them, and a strip of narrow tape fastened between them. The heads of the flowers were put to, as it were, ride astride the tight-rope, kept as close together as possible in the middle of the tape.

"TISTY TOSSTY, TELL ME TRUE, WHOM SHALL I BE MARRIED TO?"

Then came the exciting moment – we all held our breath – while the two ends were very carefully untied from the chairs, brought together, knotted, and pulled tight: there was a cowslip ball!

I never remember a failure to achieve this, but the tying is a delicate operation requiring steady hands and a cool head. After another knot or two and a snip with the scissors to remove the long ends of tape, my sister and I were ready to tell our fortunes with these flower balls, throwing them up into the air and batting – not catching – them, chanting: "Tisty tossty, tell me true, whom shall I be married to?"

"Tisty tossty" seemed to be another name for cowslip ball.— Elizabeth Steward

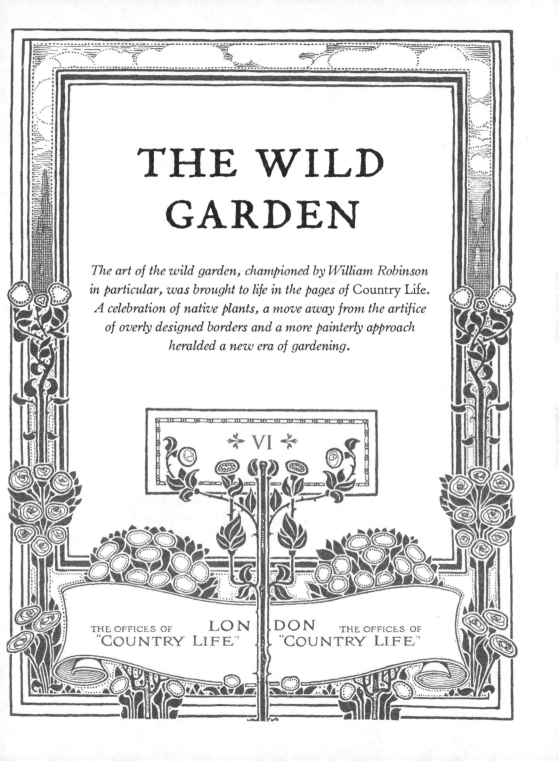

THE WILD GARDEN

The art of the wild garden, championed by William Robinson in particular, was brought to life in the pages of Country Life. *A celebration of native plants, a move away from the artifice of overly designed borders and a more painterly approach heralded a new era of gardening.*

❖ VI ❖

THE OFFICES OF
"COUNTRY LIFE"

LONDON

THE OFFICES OF
"COUNTRY LIFE"

MARCH 29TH, 1930

SAVING WILD FLOWERS

TO THE EDITOR OF "COUNTRY LIFE."

SIR,—A new society has just been formed for the protection of wild flowers and plants, and we are anxious to interest all and sundry in its work and aims.

Every day we receive accounts of destruction and extermination. To give a few examples:

A lady in Devonshire tells us her woods are being ruined by the stealing of fern fronds, apparently cut by moonlight and carted away in truckloads. A man who owns a little wood full of primroses, in Surrey, met a gipsy one morning on the way to the railway station with a perambulator full of primrose roots. And another man writes that in Cheltenham, for the last few years, fritillaries are brought in baskets 3 ft. across and astounding numbers are hawked in the streets. We have also heard of bluebell and primrose woods completely destroyed. Unless the lovers of flowers and of the beauty of the countryside will bestir themselves and help to form a really powerful society, it will soon be too late to save the flowers in the localities where they were once most abundant. Can we not learn to look on the whole country as one beautiful boundless garden and to insist that it be guarded and kept in its original loveliness? Particulars of the society can be obtained from me or, preferably, from the hon. secretary, Mr. Cyril Harding, at 31, The Avenue, Kew Gardens.—MABEL ONSLOW

> "CAN WE NOT LEARN TO LOOK ON THE WHOLE COUNTRY AS ONE BEAUTIFUL BOUNDLESS GARDEN?"

AUGUST 28ᵀᴴ, 1932

DESTRUCTION OF WILD FLOWERS

A Country Life *correspondent gives the County and District Councils a severe dressing down over their destruction of rare wild plants.*

To the Editor of "Country Life."

Sir,—Some of the worst offenders in the destruction of wild flowers are now some of the County and District Councils. Not content with having cut back the roadway until there is no flower border left, these have a mania for keeping the banks so "tidy" that they are rapidly exterminating many of the wild flowers that are left to us.

> "NATURAL BEAUTY APPEARS TO FIND NO FAVOUR WITH CORPORATIONS"

The Council here (Berriew, Montgomeryshire) is one of the worst, as all banks are trimmed, not only once a year, but kept clear. Such beautiful wild flowers as the *Geranium pyrenaicum* and the nettle-leaved bellflower (this in full flower), which we were, a short while ago, congratulating on escaping the previous mowing, have now been ruthlessly destroyed.

There is little enough natural beauty now left in this country, and such as there is appears to find no favour with Corporations. It may be advisable to remove brambles, docks and nettles, but why cannot orders be given to spare the rest?—H. H. Haines

JUNE 11TH, 1932

THE LOVE OF WILD FLOWERS

WHEN ELIZABETH WAS Queen, Gerard the herbalist took his walks from "a village hard by London called Knightsbridge, unto Fulham a village thereby," and noted that "in the fields of Holborne neare unto Gray's Inn," clary flourished, and that on Hampstead Heath, lilies of the valley, the rare white-flowered betony, devil's bit, and whortleberries abounded.

But the denudation of Hampstead Heath is an example of what happens to a tract of wild country that, through the course of centuries, is systematically cropped of its flowers.

> "AS A MAN REAPS,
> SO MUST HE SOW"

The love of flowers is almost universal, and it is the natural impulse to possess oneself of whatever pleases. But when this pleasure and this impulse are indulged by millions of persons for years on end, it can but result in the gradual extermination of the source of the pleasure. The remedy (short of enforcing a prohibition on gathering flowers, which would be intolerable) seems to lie in education, which has been successfully applied to the sublimation of other natural impulses into honourable activities.

The first obstacle to be surmounted is the ignorant assumption that if a thing is "wild," its supply is inexhaustible. The lesson – essentially one of responsibility – must be that as a man reaps, so must he sow. In schools, prizes could perhaps be offered for the cultivation of local wild flowers from seed collected; not, as so frequently occurs, for the collection of picked flowers or roots. Then, when the seedlings were ready, there could be expeditions organised to denuded places and hedgerows where the children would plant them out. For the wholesale picking of flowers by local children for sale to passers-by or export to the London markets is surely indefensible.

SEPTEMBER 14ᵀᴴ, 1940

THE NEW HERB GATHERERS

BY ENID BLYTON

Enid Blyton started a campaign to encourage schoolchildren to pick wild plants for medicinal purposes. With the need now acute, she issues a call to arms to readers of Country Life.

MANY YEARS AGO, the women and children from every country village and hamlet went out into the hills and fields to seek for many rare and common weeds, and from the dried herbs and roots, ointments, lotions, medicines and simples of all kinds were produced. Now history repeats itself. We need the herbs badly. This practice has rather fallen by the wayside, but here is a chance to wander around our countryside, to learn many of our common but valuable weeds, and to gather them in bulk so that we may help our hospital supplies and lessen the pain of many a wounded man or woman.

> "HERE IS A CHANCE TO LESSEN THE PAIN OF MANY A WOUNDED MAN OR WOMAN"

I have had the privilege of starting this nation-wide campaign in the schools of Britain. Already thousands of children are collecting the gay ragwort that is such a pest to farmers, taking the valuable seeds of the foxgloves, gathering the button-headed tansy, pulling the red clover tops, and looking for the coltsfoot leaves.

The following are a few of the medicinal herbs most urgently wanted, from which are made extremely valuable drugs.

Meadow Saffron (*Colchicum autumnale*), for instance, is in great demand – both root and seed are wanted. We often grow this in our gardens in small quantities, but it may be found locally in big stretches, the mauve (or sometimes white) crocus-like flowers springing up alone.

And the ripe black seeds of the Foxglove (*Digitalis purpurea*), the leaves of the poisonous thorn-apple (*Datura stramonium*), and even the petals of the common red poppy (*Papaver rhoeas*) and of the ordinary marigold (*Calendula officinalis*) would be most gratefully received.

Deadly Nightshade (*Atropa Belladonna*).—The most deadly plant in the kingdom. It is not common, but may be found among old ruins or quarries. Every part of it is very poisonous. Wear gloves to pluck it. The plant grows 3 ft. to 4 ft. high, and has solitary bell-shaped flowers, in colour a dingy purple. The leaves are large and egg-shaped. The fruit looks like large purple-black cherries, and these are deadly poisonous. The leaves only are wanted. They must be properly dried. (One word of warning – most people confuse the deadly nightshade with the woody nightshade, or bittersweet, and think that the latter is the deadly. Remember that the deadly nightshade has solitary dingy purple flowers, quite unlike the bright purple clusters of the woody nightshade with their distinctive yellow cone of anthers.)

Henbane (*Hyoscyamus Niger*).—The leaves of this extremely poisonous plant are most urgently needed. It is common on waste ground, especially near the sea. It is a stout plant, growing 2 ft. to 3 ft., and the large leaves are hairy and sticky. The dirty yellow flowers are funnel-shaped, purple-veined, with a dark eye, and are arranged in a double row down one side of the stem. The plant has a most offensive smell. The leaves must be properly dried.

THE NEW HERB GATHERERS

(*Left*) DEADLY NIGHTSHADE
(Atropa Belladonna)

(*Right*) HENBANE (Hyoscyamus Niger)

MARCH 15ᵀᴴ, 1946

THE WILD PASSION FLOWER

How could anyone have resisted trying to learn this correspondent's jealously guarded secret?

To the Editor of "Country Life."

Sir,—Somewhere within the triangle formed by Tring–Aldbury–Ivinghoe, on the northern borders of Hertfordshire, lies a little patch (about 100 yards in circumference) whereon grows the wild passion flower with purple petals and golden heart. It is one of only three patches of the sort in England, I believe.

"KEEP THE INFORMATION A CLOSE SECRET FROM PREDATORY MOTORISTS"

This secret was entrusted to me thirty-five years ago. But as neither of my two daughters can (through no fault of their own) benefit by knowledge of the exact position of the patch, I am anxious to find a family of naturalists to whom I can pass on the information, secure in the knowledge that they will (a) keep the information a close secret from predatory motorists, and (b) will never dig up and remove the plants from their beautiful natural setting.

If, therefore, any of your readers are desirous of learning this secret, I shall be glad to reveal it to such of them as can satisfy me that they seek no personal gain other than the pleasure which comes from studying Nature.—P. A. Chubb

JUNE 27ᵀᴴ, 1925

A HILLSIDE GARDEN

To the Editor of "Country Life."

Sir,—One of the problems of a garden on a steep incline is the covering of its banks. The garden here depicted has two very steep banks, with a narrow grass terrace between. They face south and are so steep and dry that even weeds find an insecure lodging. First attempts to clothe them failed, but later a few ox-eyed daisies sprang up, seeding themselves freely year by year till they covered the dry, bare banks in sheets of dazzling white, with the dark firs providing a most effective background.— G. Walton

BULBOUS PLANTS IN GRASS AND WOODLAND

By Gertrude Jekyll

I F THE SPACE for planting is not large, it would be well to stick to two or three kinds of bulbous plants only, such as the fine trumpets *Horsfieldii*, *Emperor* and *Rugilobus*. But if the space is large, extending over some acres, there is an opportunity for planting in a proper sequence of many kinds and each kind in fair quantity.

Thus, beginning at one end, one would start by planting the trumpets. Then would follow the fine Sir Watkin, the *incomparabilis* (and their hybrids, the *Leedsii* and *Barri* varieties), and then the *Poeticus*, both double and single.

Some of the cheapest bulbs are among the most effective. In the case of *incomparabilis*, the higher-priced kinds with the strong coloured cups are fine in the hand but actually less beautiful in the mass. It is better to look for the more even colour of cup and perianth, so as not to interfere with breadth of effect.

The manner of the actual planting is of importance. Instead of planting in roundish patches, it is much better in the case of all bulbs for wild gardening to plant in long-shaped drifts, as shown in the sketch, the drifts all running in one direction, and being so placed in relation to paths or the more obvious points of view that they are seen from any of the ways indicated by the arrows. The advantage of such planting in pictorial

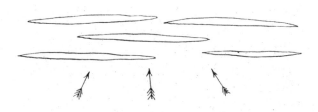

effect is quite incontestable,. and in the case of Daffodils, seen, under the low yellow sunlight of a spring afternoon, an harmonious quality of the highest artistic value is obtained. The same rule of planting applies equally to the smaller spring bulbs—Crocuses, Winter Aconites, Snowdrops, Dogs'-tooth Violets, *Scillas* and *Chionodoxas*. Snowdrops and Winter Aconites are beautiful in groves of large trees where the ground is bare beneath. Winter Aconite succeeds almost anywhere, even under Beeches, and increases quickly by self-sown seed. Snowdrops do best in soils that are either loamy or calcareous. Grape Hyacinths (*Muscari*) flower with the later Daffodils. The fine form of *Muscari conicum* called Heavenly Blue is easily naturalised, and has a fine effect when in good quantity. By the second week of May there are Trilliums, beautiful by themselves in cool woodland and rejoicing in deep beds of leaf-mould. At the same season there should be, in damp turf in the open, two of the most beautiful of our native plants, the tall Summer Snowflake (*Leucojum aestivum*) and the Snake's-head Fritillary. If there is a stretch of grass that is almost boggy, these two plants will be seen at their best, the Snowflake revelling in the wettest part.

> "THE ADVANTAGE OF SUCH PLANTING IN PICTORIAL EFFECT IS QUITE INCONTESTABLE ..."

For the later year there are still some beautiful bulbous plants for wild gardening. First the Autumn *Colchicum*, best in chalky soils, but good anywhere except in the poorest sand. The type *Colchicum autumnale* that is the most desirable in meadow land, and it is in grass that it not only thrives best, but also receives the support to the weak-stemmed bloom—not a true stem, but an elongated tube—that is necessary to keep it upright. In drier ground, in short, fine turf, should be planted the beautiful *Crocus speciosus*, like *Colchicum*, blooming in September and October, and increasing fast by self-sown seed. For the same season, in thin grass at the foot of trees and in the edges of woodland, there should be tufts of hardy Cyclamens.

OCTOBER 3ʳᵈ, 1914

AN AUTUMN FLOWER BED

BY GERTRUDE JEKYLL

WITH THE PASSING of summer and the advent of cold nights, the value of those varieties capable of withstanding the ravages of Nature is more fully appreciated. Too often the many beautiful hardy plants suitable for filling large beds are overlooked, a point that was brought home to me rather forcibly last year by a large lawn bed filled with dwarf blue Michaelmas Daisies and white Japanese Anemones, or Windflowers. The first named were plants of *Aster amellus bessarabicus*, which grows not more than 18 in. high, and produced quite a carpet with its large and intensely blue flowers. The Japanese Anemones reached a height of 3 ft. 6 in. The effect of white and blue was exceedingly charming, and a bed such as this would not be at all costly. Earlier in the year, Daffodils, thinly planted between the perennials, created a gold and white effect, and these were followed at the end of June and early July with dark blue Spanish Irises. By adopting this system of planting, the bed was a source of interest over a period of at least six months, and needed very little attention.

SEPTEMBER 14TH, 1897

WILD GARDENING

The wild garden is something that, though now more widely spread,
was very particular to England – the art of harnessing, without overly
restraining, nature.

WILD GARDENING TAKES many forms. It is not only the large garden with broad woodlands that offers opportunities for planting the Daffodil and many other bulbous flowers, but also smaller gardens, where the Solomon's Seal, Daffodil and *Scilla* can be used to brighten shrubbery borders or fringe some shady walk. It is not unusual to find Solomon's Seal in town gardens, planted amongst hardy ferns and Spanish *Scillas*.

⁂

A VALUABLE NOTE FROM MR. ROBINSON: "The prettiest results are attainable only where the grass need not be cut till the meadows are mown. Then we may have gardens of Narcissi such as no one ever thought possible in Britain. In grass not mown at all we may even enjoy many of the Lilies and the other lovely and stately bulbous flowers of Europe, Asia and America. Copses and woods offer still better situations, as here there is no destruction of the foliage by harrow, roller or mower. All planting in the grass should be in natural groups or prettily fringed colonies, growing to and fro as they like. Lessons in these grouping are to be learned in the woods, copses, heaths and meadows by those who look about them as they go. Once established, the plants soon begin to group themselves in pretty ways."

MAY 15TH, 1915

THE WILD GARDEN OVERDONE

BY WILLIAM ROBINSON

*William Robinson was, of course, one of the key figures in the
development of the wild garden. Here Mr. Robinson advises on
the planting of bulbs.*

THE WILD WAY OF adorning a lawn, orchard or garden is, especially in the spring, often overdone, and many examples may be seen of roots set thickly and flowers covering the whole of the ground. On a lawn mown twice a year for hay it does very well, but on the whole it is a mistake.

When planting Narcissi in grass to be mown for hay, take care to lightly plant. At Kew, at first, and in some public gardens, the flowers were planted like tiles on a roof and their charm was altogether lost.

> "THE TROUBLE YOU HAD IN GETTING THEM IN WILL BE SMALL COMPARED TO GETTING THEM OUT"

Narcissi increase so rapidly that it becomes very difficult to thin them out. The late Mr. F. W. Burbidge, who knew the Narcissi well, once said, on seeing my plantings, "The trouble you had in getting them in will be small compared to getting them out."

It is much better to plant as with the scarlet Windflower – less easily acquired than other bulbs and so usually tried, to immense advantage, in small quantities.

JULY 12TH, 1930

PLANT HUNTING ON THE EDGE OF THE WORLD: IN SEARCH OF THE RARE WILD FLOWER

BY CAPTAIN F. KINGDON WARD

THE BOLD MOUNTAIN range that shuts off Assam from Eastern Tibet is a wild exotic garden with a powerful attraction for the plant hunter. Sanction to travel in this unadministered territory is only very rarely granted by the Government of India but this, and other obstacles, have been instrumental in keeping the region inviolate.

"IN HARSH DESOLATION, THE MOST WONDERFUL OF ALL ALPINES SMOULDER IN THE SMOKING MIST"

My companion and I camped in the rain forest at the end of May and prepared to explore the alps for plants. Above the last cultivation, the rain forest begins, and at 9,000 ft. this passes into a rhododendron conifer forest which, at 11,000 ft., in turn gives way to solid forests of silver fir. At 12,000 ft., tree growth ceases, replaced by rhododendron scrub and alpine meadow above which is only bare rock and barren scree. It is in this alpine region that the chief interest for the botanist lies.

Here, in harsh desolation, the dwarf scarlet rhododendrons – the most wonderful of all alpines and the treasure of the Mishmi Hills – smoulder in the smoking mist. They cower, fathoms deep, beneath a snow quilt for seven months of the year, untroubled by the howling wind which spins off the surface in spirals of powdered glass. Whenever a rare shaft of sunshine drives through the huddled clouds, the flowers gleam and glitter like jewels.

JUNE 10TH, 1922

SHRUBS FOR A WOODLAND GARDEN

BY J. G. MILLAIS

J. G. Millais writes most astutely on why trial and error are so important to the success and pleasure of the gardener.

IT IS NECESSARY that the owner-gardener should make a careful study of plants, including what they will eventually become, before commencing planting operations. It is essential to keep in mind what the garden will be like in twenty or thirty years' time if he succeeds according to his highest hopes.

> "THOUGH WE MAKE THE MOST COLOSSAL MISTAKES, THE MERE FACT OF DOING THINGS ONESELF IN A GARDEN IS A CONTINUOUS SOURCE OF PLEASURE"

Most gardeners are far too modest in this respect and allow too much for what they imagine will be failures. Consequently, they are apt to plant the permanent plants – magnolias, various fine species of *Cornus*, Japanese maples, *Stuartias*, *Eucryphias*, etc., all of which blend exquisitely with rhododendrons – too close together or too near the front of the border. Other shrubs, such as rhododendrons and camellias, can be moved at a later date, but not so with the aforementioned permanents.

It is a platitude that, even though we make the most colossal mistakes, the mere fact of doing things oneself in a garden is a continuous source of pleasure. Some mistakes can be corrected in time, and others stare us in the face for life, but on balance we reap so much joy from the successful issue of our plans that errors do not matter so much after all.

Few men and women are altogether devoid of artistic sense and it is, in the end, better to muddle through the severe school of experience than to employ those who often possess only stereotyped views. I must confess to an abiding distrust of the professional layer-out of gardens. Too often they have but a trifling knowledge of plants and shrubs and are only bent on spending money on "garden architecture." We should all aim at originality and self-expression, for without that we become soulless invertebrates.

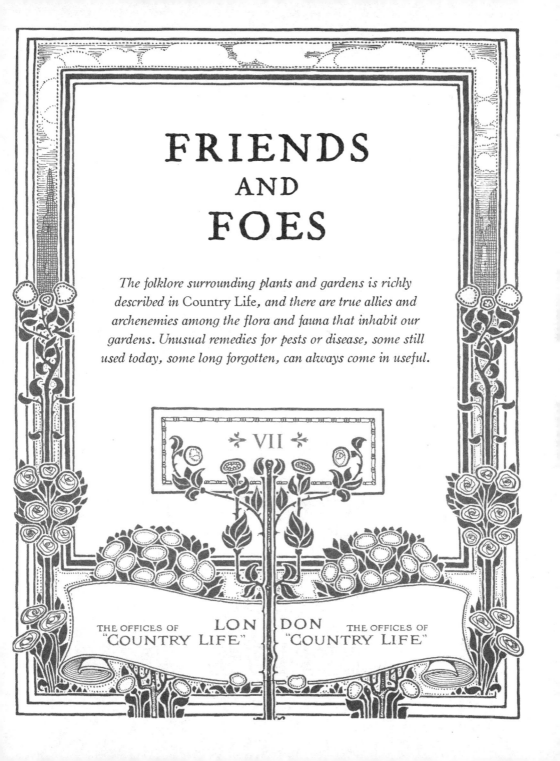

FRIENDS AND FOES

The folklore surrounding plants and gardens is richly described in Country Life*, and there are true allies and archenemies among the flora and fauna that inhabit our gardens. Unusual remedies for pests or disease, some still used today, some long forgotten, can always come in useful.*

VII

THE OFFICES OF "COUNTRY LIFE" LONDON THE OFFICES OF "COUNTRY LIFE"

SEPTEMBER 12TH, 1914

GARDEN PESTS: A MIXED BAG!

To the Editor of "Country Life."

Sir,—Finding that the peaches and pears on my wall trees were being badly nibbled before they were ripe, I set three penny mousetraps of the "break back" kind and, in just a few days, I have had the following "bag": thirteen field voles, three long-tailed field mice, one house mouse, one sparrow, three large slugs, one snail, one toad, four robins, one frog, and one newt. The bait was half an almond glued on to the trap. The last four items are to be regretted, but robins have a habit of poking their inquisitive beaks into everything and their young are very destructive to small fruit. The voles were probably the chief offenders, and after this clearance the fruit remains untouched.—M. Robinson

> "THE VOLES WERE PROBABLY THE CHIEF OFFENDERS"

AUGUST 22ND, 1936

THE FATE OF A SNAIL

To the Editor of "Country Life."

Sir,—Books of reference on gardening all agree that slugs and snails are two of the gardener's greatest enemies: "Nothing with a soft, sappy stem is proof against their attacks."

Yesterday I came across what I should imagine is a unique example of this. A young foxglove was apparently broken through about halfway up the stem, the top half bending down but not quite touching the ground. In the angle thus formed was a large black snail, most securely held. Upon lifting up the stem, the reason became apparent. The snail had eaten through the stem, and was still eating when it fell. The "jaws" formed by the edges of the hole had closed around the mouth and adjacent parts of the snail – a curious snail-trap! So tight was the hold that the flesh was almost cut through, giving the snail a false head and creating a creature with remarkable resemblance to a miniature tortoise. Curiously enough, the foxglove was growing in a cemetery.—
George C. Paluster

MARCH 1ST, 1941

BEES IN THE GARDEN

OUR ANCESTORS NEVER had to worry about the sugar shortage; the beehives that stood in homely rows in the gardens of rich and poor provided them with all the sweets they needed. "Plant More Potatoes!" and "Eat More Carrots!" urge our anxious Ministries of Food. And they would be wise to add, "Keep more bees in the garden!"

To quote from a report from the Ministry of Agriculture, honey is completely digestible: one pound of it has the calorific value of thirty eggs or three pints of milk. Honey is a sovereign remedy for fatigue: as a heat producer worth twice its weight of butter it is a useful substitute for cod liver oil, a better restorative for the heart than alcohol, and invaluable for healing throat and chest. But it must be real honey, gathered by real bees from real flowers – not the synthetic stuff made by man in imitation honeycombs.

"BEES ARE EXQUISITELY DAINTY AND HATE DIRT AND DISAGREEABLE ODOURS"

Bee-keeping is a simple craft, but not simple enough to teach in one short article: it is possible only to advise, relate personal experience, and utter a few warnings.

A good hand-book on the subject is the first step; next, a visit to a bee-keeper in the neighbourhood. He is sure to welcome you, for all bee-masters are brothers. He will tell you how to get reliable stock – perhaps he will even provide it himself – and lend you his skep, smoker, extractor, and all the equipment the amateur usually acquires by degrees.

The best month to start bees is March, for with good luck and a good bee-master that means honey the same year. But if March is impossible, the amateur might get his hive, either new or second-hand, in readiness, and wait until the bee-keeper can supply him with a swarm in late May or early June.

The bees will arrive in a skep or travelling-box, and this must be placed in a shady spot until sundown, when they may be hived. If a second-hand hive is used, it must have been thoroughly cleaned and disinfected. Bees are exquisitely dainty and hate dirt and disagreeable odours. And, like the bee-masters of old who raised their hats to the hive in passing, we must respect their wishes.

JUNE 2ND, 1923

FLOWER SUPERSTITIONS

To the Editor of "Country Life."

SIR,—Country folk have the strangest superstitions, and their superstitions relative to flowers and trees are, I think, the most interesting. For instance, to bring a sprig of wild thyme, gorse, blackthorn, or even the bright-hued wild poppy into the house is an unlucky omen, predicting illness and even death. In some parts of England, to sow fennel or parsley seed is indicative of bad luck. And should spring flowers blossom in autumn, the country folk shake their heads and quote the old proverb: "A green Yule makes a fat churchyard."

Should a piece of yellow broom be brought into the house in May, death is sure to enter that house. The harmless little buttercup which flecks the fields with gold is also, we learn, unlucky – to even smell this flower produces madness. The dainty little snowdrop and primrose, too, are unlucky if only a single flower is carried into the house when first they come into bloom. And if we should spy thistledown floating in the air when there is no wind, we may be certain it will rain before long.

But who does not know that a pea pod containing nine peas is the best of luck? The same with the four-leaved clover, although these can scarcely be called flowers. A holly tree burdened with berries prognosticates a hard winter, while a bay tree in the garden is a sure preventative against death and the devil. But, mark my words, should the said tree wither, then the death of someone in the house is surely foretold.—LETTY LAIDLAW

THE HAPPY GARDENER

WHAT HOSTS OF enemies encompass the gardener! How they mass for a simultaneous attack on all fronts, eating their way in with tooth and beak, battering garden produce, and multiplying at a terrific rate. Slugs and snails, though slow, are too good at their field craft for me and it's only the most unwary that I manage to kill. Worms may work wonders in beds, but on the lawn they're a pest. I wormed it this year with a powder whose inventor proclaimed on the tin: "This worm-killer is infallible and the worms will immediately come up in swarms ready to be swept up." But it was just as infallible as most things in this mortal life and, though I waited for days with broom at the ready, only three worms came up from a lawn all crumbly with casts.

Birds defeat me. Bullfinches look so jolly, perched in the fruit trees like tubby guardsmen in bear skins, that I haven't the heart (or skill) to shoot them. Once, with much stalking, I shot a Jay, but did it so badly I vowed never to try again. The blackbird I spare for his song, which is sweet as the fruit he eats.

All these and the rats – animal and human – who raid my fruit are on my black-list and will be openly fought.

Then there's the friend turned foe. The dog is a sedate connoisseur of flowers till the holidays come, when he loses all garden sense and chases cricket balls, hockey balls, tennis balls, and footballs all over the beds. And the baby, once content to pick daisies, begins to pick polyanthus and wallflowers.

The hens sometimes escape, as only prisoners behind wire know how to, and attack everything green within sight with murderous beak and claw, strewing the paths with debris. Already the wretched poultry-keeper spends so much time away from gardening on their feeding, cleaning and guarding at Christmas that it is clear why the author of my poultry manual calls it *Eggs From the Garden*.

Worst of all is the gardener himself. Though I hide the necessary weapons from him, he yearly trims the *forsythia* so that it flowers out of reach: an ex-woodman, he loves felling trees, and cut down our only damson, in its prime, to provide a pole for the washing line. Having dug to death my wife's lily-of-the-valley bed he said to her with a grin: "Now you can scratch away there to your 'eart's content with your little trowel." He must, I feel, be the scapegoat of all gardeners since the days of Adam. But, as the family says, he's "wizard on birds."

"WHAT HOSTS OF ENEMIES ENCOMPASS THE GARDENER!"

But it is worth it, a hundred times over. I am a happy gardener. — G. RIDSDILL SMITH

JULY 17ᵀᴴ, 1942

WORMS AND VIBRATION

To THE EDITOR OF "COUNTRY LIFE."

Sɪʀ,—Many years ago, some small boys came to play in my Hampstead garden. Having no toys with them, but never at a loss to find amusement, they took some empty flower-pots and placed them in a row on the lawn, with the object of producing a complete musical scale by tapping the pots with a stick. This took some little time and much tapping to accomplish. At the end, the children called to me to come and see what had happened, and on going to them I found – much to my astonishment, and theirs – that numbers of worms had come to the surface of the lawn around the pots.—Iʀᴇɴᴇ M. Iʀᴏɴsɪᴅᴇ

JULY 17TH, 1942

A GARDENER'S FRIEND

An undervalued ally of the gardener, the slow-worm is here enlisted as a recruit in the Dig For Victory campaign.

To the Editor of "Country Life."

SIR,—Many people have an instinctive dislike for any creature that is snakelike and, in consequence, the slow-worm is often killed.

However, it is neither a snake nor a worm, but a legless lizard. Its skin is smooth and shiny, and quite pleasant to touch. It is an extremely good friend of the gardener, as it greedily devours those greyish slugs which are such pests.

It changes (or "sloughs") its skin, and its present name may be a corruption of "slough-worm". The alternative name of blind-worm is also inappropriate, since this lizard has a good pair of eyes, and also two pairs of eyelids.

In the summer it gives birth to about half a dozen youngsters, and almost as soon as they are born they can look after themselves. These interesting and valuable reptiles deserve every encouragement, especially in these days when every vegetable is precious.—JOHN H. VICKERS

Left: The Slow-Worm – an "extremely good friend of the gardener".

NOVEMBER 18ᵀᴴ, 1939

PURGED

To the Editor of "Country Life."

Sir,—Two young evacuees who were suddenly taken ill after returning from a recent afternoon's blackberrying considerably puzzled those responsible for them when, in answer to the question as to what they had been eating, they replied: "Only some blackberries and black-currants!" The suggestion that black-currant bushes are to be found bearing fruit in late October, in Gloucestershire, was intriguing, so a day or two later, when the children had recovered, the writer asked them to show him where these bushes were. A half-hour's walk found us in a narrow overgrown lane, and suddenly two shrill young voices proclaimed: "There's the currant tree, Mister!" and two small hands pointed straight at a fair specimen of *Rhamnus cathartica*, better known as "purging buckthorn."

Once it was made clear to them that these were only "imitation currants," and the cause of their recent sufferings, the youngsters promised to be more wary in future. Further questioning elicited the information that, while they did not like the taste very much, "You didn't notice it if you swallowed them quick like." In short, swallowed whole, like pills. A branch of the buckthorn was brought home and this photograph taken.—L. M.

FEBRUARY 2ND, 1924

RABBIT-PROOF PLANTS

TO THE EDITOR OF "COUNTRY LIFE."

SIR,—Of all the long lists of rabbit-proof plants ever published, I find that my species of rabbits can somehow eat and appreciate practically all of them. A friend of mine once published a very exhaustive list of rabbit-proof plants, and I feel certain he never has regretted any publication more sincerely in his life, for rabbits are always cropping up and eating said plants and, just as surely, indignant letters from their owners result. It is with not a little timidity that I make this suggestion, but I really think the following four plants are rabbit-proof: Boxwood, *philadelphus*, *hypericum* and *nepeta*.

I fondly thought I had discovered another in the *Buddleia* family, but my experiences were as follows. I planted five plants of *Buddleia variabilis* in the spring of 1922. They were not interfered with by rabbits in any way – not even a leaf was sampled – neither through that summer nor the following winter. So, firmly believing that I had discovered a truly rabbit-proof plant, I very considerably increased my clump

"CAN ANY OF YOUR READERS EXPLAIN HOW THE BRUTES KNEW THE DIFFERENCE?"

by planting quite a number more, taken from precisely the same nursery stock as those already planted. But – would you believe? – in the course of ten days the rabbits had eaten every vestige of the newcomers, although they paid not the slightest attention to the five original plants which came, as I have already said, from the same nursery patch. Can any of your readers explain how the brutes knew the difference?—FORMAKIN

AUGUST 18ᵀᴴ, 1923

BLACKBIRDS AND GARDEN PEAS

Editors of Country Life *took great pains to submit queries to a relevant expert. Here a despairing gardener receives a surprising and not immediately practical solution to his blackbird problem.*

To the Editor of "Country Life."

Sir,—Of all the wild birds, the blackbird is the one for which I used to have the greatest friendship. But I am afraid that it will not be possible to put up for very long with the new habits it has acquired. The worst of these is a pernicious taste for green peas.

"EITHER THEY OR THE VEGETABLE GARDEN WILL HAVE TO GO"

They have become experts in the fine art of shelling them. With the bill for a chisel they cut into the pod, extract the peas nearest the opening, and then enlarge it until all the contents can be grabbed.

Gentle means of scaring them have been tried, in vain, by the gardener. They pass through nets, pay no heed to threads either white or black, and evidently regard paper and rags as having been hung up to fan them.

I have been wondering whether any of your readers could suggest a means of preventing their depredations. Comparatively stern measures might benefit them in the end, because if they carry their robbery further, either they or the vegetable garden will have to go.

One would rather not have to speak in such terms, but these are the bare bones of the situation.—PEASCOD

[This letter was submitted to Dr. Walter E. Collinge, who writes: "In the past, the number of blackbirds has been kept in check by boys collecting their eggs, and it would be well if the hobby were revived. No one wishes to see wild birds wantonly destroyed, but that their numbers must be held in check is obvious."—Ed]

OCTOBER 21ST, 1916
WOODLICE IN MELON FRAME

TO THE EDITOR OF "COUNTRY LIFE."

SIR,—In reply to your correspondent on "Woodlice in Melon Frame," if he got a common toad and put it in his frame, he would clear it in a very few days. I had the same nuisance some years ago and applied the above remedy. In a few days my frame was quite clear of them and all other insects.—JAMES TURNER

"IF HE GOT A COMMON TOAD AND PUT IT IN HIS FRAME"

AUGUST 15TH, 1903

FERN LORE

Where the copsewood is the greenest,
Where the fountains glisten sheenest,
Where the morning dew lies longest,
There the Lady-fern grows strongest.—Scott

LIKE THE FAR-FAMED ring of Gyges, fern-seed is traditionally supposed to possess the power of rendering its owner invisible and enabling him to detect all witches disguised in the human shape. But to be endued with these properties, the seed must be caught upon a plate as it falls from the buckler fern at midnight upon Midsummer's Eve – the precise moment of that already-mystic night when, it is said, St. John the Baptist was born. Upon Midsummer's Day, charms, known as "lucky-hands" or "St. John's hands", were often woven from the curled-in fronds of the buckler fern, as these were supposed to impart a peculiar virtue to cattle troughs.

In the days of the Stuarts, the root of the male fern was much used by maidens in their preparation of love potions, although her lover might be reluctant to acknowledge the real means by which he had been enthralled:

'Twas the maiden's matchless beauty,
That drew my heart a-nigh,
Not the fern-root potion,
But the glance of her blue eye.

The brake fern, or "bracken" as it is more usually termed, is said to send up a small blue flower every year on Michaelmas Eve at midnight. This blossom, however, always disappears at dawn. Upon the Continent, the peasants claim that this flower possesses similar powers to those of the divining-rod, although it indicates hidden treasures, and not springs of water. Shepherds declare that it can also point out the whereabouts of strayed flocks.

In Staffordshire, there is an old belief that the burning of large tracts of bracken is sure to bring on heavy rains. Ahead of his visit to the county, King Charles I even ordered a letter to be sent to the Sheriff of Staffordshire strictly prohibiting such an act:

"Sir,—His Majesty, taking notice of an opinion entertained in Staffordshire that the burning of ferne doth draw down rain, and being desirous that the country and himself may enjoy fair weather so long as he remains in these parts, His Majesty has commanded me to write to you to cause all burning of ferne to be forborne, until His Majesty be passed the country."

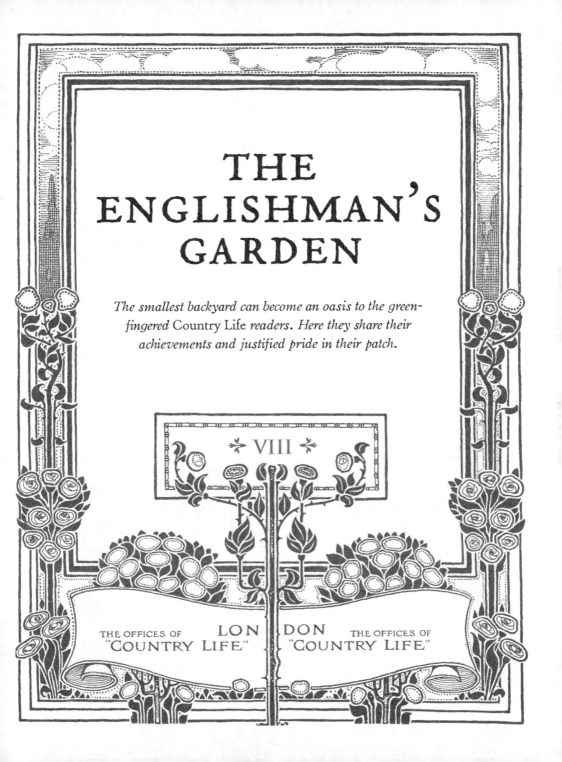

THE ENGLISHMAN'S GARDEN

The smallest backyard can become an oasis to the green-fingered Country Life *readers. Here they share their achievements and justified pride in their patch.*

✽ VIII ✽

THE OFFICES OF LONDON THE OFFICES OF
"COUNTRY LIFE" "COUNTRY LIFE"

JUNE 18ᵀᴴ, 1927

A GARDEN IN YUKON

To the Editor of "Country Life."

Sir,—I have just received the enclosed photograph from near the Arctic circle, in the Yukon territory of Canada. The border shown is only one-sixth of its size and is one of four. The owner of this beautiful garden – which includes Delphiniums 11 ft. tall – is English, and people come 100 miles to see "an old English garden." From November to May, it lies under snow.—FLORA PILKINGTON

"PEOPLE COME 100 MILES TO SEE 'AN OLD ENGLISH GARDEN'"

SEPTEMBER 5ᵀᴴ, 1931

LONDON GARDENS

THE ENGLISHMAN HAS a genuine and deep-seated instinct for making a garden – not just a cabbage patch, but a place gay with flowers, for the English are a nation of countrymen and London is not really a city but a colossal village. Our efforts at city planning are desultory and unsuccessful, and we seem not to have it in us to submit to the discipline that has created the grandiose capitals of the Continent. But, also unlike the town dwellers of the Continent, a huge proportion of Londoners can produce a merry-faced garden of their own, notably reflected in their own visages.

This is an exceedingly psychological fact. The artisan possessed of a house of his own, with a plot of ground in which to express himself, takes a very different view of life from one who is the tenant of a municipality in a block of tall dwellings, without any contact with the soil. Our policy of building houses with gardens not only meets a deep-seated national demand, but gives people homes in the English conception of the term.

Up until now even the Bank of England has had its own garden – most refreshing to the jaded eyes of successive Governors. But the re-building of the bank heralds the destruction of the garden, and similar situations are seen in many congested areas.

"FOR THE ENGLISH ARE A NATION OF COUNTRYMEN"

The loss of garden space in the more crowded slum areas could to some extent be counteracted by making gardens of a kind on the roofs. Enormous areas are wasted in London by the antipathy to flat roofs – a tenet of rustic conservatism that particularly strikes our American visitors. Recently, a party of American architects being shown around the new British Embassy in Washington asked their host about the English disposition for "ruddy fingers" on the roof. They were referring, of course, to our red brick chimney stacks.

JANUARY 27TH, 1934

ALLOTMENT SHEDS FOR THE UNEMPLOYED

The instinct to share new knowledge, especially if accompanied by a diagram, was almost irresistible to many Country Life *readers.*

TO THE EDITOR OF "COUNTRY LIFE."

SIR,—In view of the progress being made with the supply of allotments to the unemployed, especially by the Society of Friends, the enclosed notes may be of interest. They deal with the type of shed which is a desirable – indeed, essential – adjunct, and are based on observations made on a visit to allotments in Germany. In that country the huts are uniform and are placed at the junction of four plots. They house tools, etc., and afford a retreat in bad weather for the four plot holders.

The accompanying sketch shows the method of construction. A central post composed of four triangular sections (A, A, A, A) is set vertically into the ground to a depth of a foot. Distance pieces are inserted

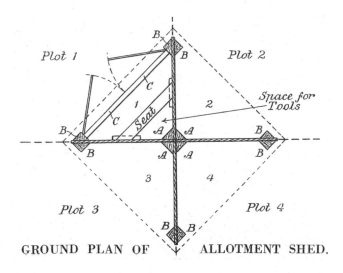

GROUND PLAN OF ALLOTMENT SHED.

to form open slots into which notched boards (say 9 ins, by ¾ inch) are slid down until a height of about 5 ft. 6 in. is built up. The triangular-sectioned pieces at the four corners (B, B) are then nailed on, and hinged double doors attached. Sills and heads (C, C) are in turn nailed on. A flat roof of sawn boards is attached and covered with rubberoid or other suitable waterproofing. Floors

> "THE TYPE OF SHED IS A DESIRABLE – INDEED, ESSENTIAL – ADJUNCT"

can be laid down using old bricks, railway sleepers, concrete, or cinders. Provision is easily made for a seat, behind which is a space for tools.— ROBERT McDOUGALL

MAY 26TH, 1944

FLOWERS FOR SHOREDITCH

TO THE EDITOR OF "COUNTRY LIFE."

SIR,—I am writing to ask whether any of your readers whose gardens are not wholly given over to vegetable growing during this war period might have any flowers to spare during the summer months. Shoreditch is a very drab district indeed, and the large numbers of children from surrounding streets who visit the Museum in their leisure time and in school parties respond enthusiastically to any displays of flowers we are able to arrange and very much appreciate these glimpses of beauty.— M. HARRISON, ACTING CURATOR, THE GEFFRYE MUSEUM

DECEMBER 9TH, 1939

AN ENGLISH GARDEN

BY G. C. TAYLOR

The 1939 World Fair in New York gives Britain a chance to show off its garden design.

FOR GENERATIONS PAST our gardens have been the admiration and envy of gardening devotees in many other countries, and the British Pavilion at the recent New York World's Fair provided just such an example. It is never an easy task to design a garden for exhibition purposes – least of all one that is to reflect national tendencies – but Mr. Percy Cane carried out his task with conspicuous skill and, as the accompanying illustration shows, succeeded in translating our underlying principles and ideas of modern garden design into a simple and admirable practical form.

"SPACIOUSNESS AND QUIET BEAUTY . . . QUALITIES THAT ARE ESSENTIALLY ENGLISH"

Lawns are perhaps the chief feature of English gardens, their feeling of spaciousness and quiet beauty being qualities that are essentially English. A flagged path, the stones of which came from Whitehall Gardens and the Tower of London, bordered the lawn. Dense green walls of thuya were planted to ensure privacy – another English quality – while pines and birches heightened further the effect of seclusion and permanence and evoked the Surrey common. Bold groups of hardy flowers afforded another typical English feature – the herbaceous border – and, arranged in a series of harmonious colours changing from soft pinks through blues and mauves to strong reds, oranges and yellows, afforded a striking display. Thousands of lily bulbs afforded picturesque incidents and reflected the increasing popularity of this aristocratic group of bulbs in recent years.

In its simple and straightforward design, in the quiet spaciousness of the mown lawn, in the richly coloured ribbon of herbaceous flowers, and in the old sundial, the garden provided a harmonious and typically English setting, as well as reflecting that strong measure of individuality which is characteristic of most of our gardening efforts.

AUGUST 11ᵀᴴ, 1944

A PRISONER'S FLOWERS

BY JOHN BUXTON

[The writer of this article, which has been delayed in transmission, is a prisoner of war in Germany, having been captured in Norway.—Ed]

Even in prison they can solace me.
For where they bloom God is, and I am free.—John Clare

THE TRODDEN COMPOUND where first we were imprisoned was barren. On some mornings we picked from the dusty ground some twisted yellow fragments of shrapnel or splinters of bombs, but never a flower was there to find. But later, in Oslo, in the small orchard where we might be out of doors, there was a bank of greater celandine, and here and there a small flower in the grass.

In Poland, on the ramparts of an old fort, were multitudinous flowers, some fragrant, and through the spring and summer of 1941, I kept a record of the flowers as they came into bloom. The "island" (for so we called this place) was thickly wooded with birch and willow, and there was one cherry tree which, though rather shadowed by neighbouring trees, put out its first blossoms on April 29th. Within a few days there were violets and aconites and daisies, and among the flowers a number of butterflies – brimstones, small tortoisehells, and at least one camberwell beauty.

"DURING THE LAST DAYS OF MAY MANY MORE FLOWERS OF ENGLISH FIELDS CAME ON THE ISLAND"

On the wall, ivy-leaved toadflax and herb robert were in flower now, and where a wooden sewer came down were stinging nettles, some sprigs of willow and elder, and brambles from which we gathered a few blackberries.

During the last days of May many more flowers of English fields came on the island – bird's foot trefoil, purple vetch, black medick and cornflower. On the last day of the month, I was looking for a dropped pencil under a seat and there, among the leaves, was a newly emerged female poplar hawk moth, with soft grey wings perfect to the last scale.

Through June we saw such handsome plants as the butterfly orchid and clustered campanula, and July brought a few spikes of mullein. On the great buttressed wall of our building, wild strawberries came into flower, and mosses and grey lichen afforded pasture for hundreds of snails – some helix, but many more Clausilia. Higher in the wall a pair of redstarts nested, and many swifts, racing in threes and fives, ran screaming along the wall.

MARCH 27TH, 1937

A VILLAGE GARDEN COMPETITION

Long before Britain in Bloom or Best-Kept Village competitions, Country Life *was encouraging a nationwide effort to enhance the appearance of our villages. The tone is perhaps patrician, but the desire for villages to dignify their modern and ancient features is hard to fault.*

THE CORONATION PLANTING Committee has suggested a nation-wide village garden competition. The Committee would present a certificate for the most attractive front garden in each village and, should enough villages enter, some permanent token, such as a seat or a village sign, for the village in each county which has made the best permanent contribution to its appearance.

A pamphlet named *The Village: How to Make and Keep It Beautiful* has many suggestions, among them the use of such easily obtainable plants as *Philadelphus erectus, Berberis Wilsoniae* and *Rosa rugosa* for hedging, and a more lavish use of colour wash for those houses and buildings built of unattractive materials. It is recommended that villages stick to coherent planting schemes, as a mixed planting of flowering trees looks better on paper than it does in fact.

"THE VILLAGE MUST GROW OR BE A MUSEUM PIECE"

The pamphlet has not forgotten the more difficult side of the picture: the removal or control of eyesores. It is not particularly the "old world" quality that the Committee would like to preserve, but rather it is anxious that all the difficulties and delights of village amenities should be tackled so that each feature – a castle ruin, the village butter cross, the water tower, petrol station or playing fields – fills its purpose with dignity. The village must grow or be a museum piece.

MARCH 27TH, 1937

LEAGUE OF FLOWER GIVERS

To the Editor of "Country Life."

Sir,—There are probably many among your readers who have not heard of the "League of Flower Givers," a simple scheme by which schools, hospitals, missions, homes, district nurses, etc., in the slums of London are sent garden flowers.

> "AFTER A PARTICULARLY GREY WINTER, THE COMING OF SPRING IS HERALDED WITH JOY"

The idea is for individuals or groups of friends to send flowers from their own garden to the place they "adopt" as regularly as possible.

This year especially, after a particularly grey winter, the coming of spring is heralded with joy. Yet there are many who will never have a glimpse of its beauty. There must be so many who would be only too glad to give them this glimpse if they knew where to send it.

I will give addresses and full particulars to anybody who is interested.—Eileen Turvill

SEPTEMBER 27TH, 1924

THE PUREST OF HUMAN PLEASURES

TO THE EDITOR OF "COUNTY LIFE."

SIR,—Cottage gardens are one of the pleasantest sights of the countryside, and ripe old age – cheerful, frugal and kindly – is another. I send you a photograph of an old woman in her garden near Richmond, Yorkshire, which I think gives a charming but not uncommon picture of both.— ELLERTON SWALL

SEPTEMBER 16ᵀᴴ, 1899

MAKING THE MOST OF IT

Mr. Foxlee, a correspondent, was justly proud of his efforts to create a miniature hanging garden in London.

To the Editor of "Country Life."

Sir,—With reference to your remarks regarding hanging gardens in London, I enclose a photograph of the method by which I utilise the little space I have at command. I have, unfortunately, no garden at the back of my house, and my yard is of very limited area, but I nevertheless manage to "farm" some nine or ten fowls, and also taste the joy brought by a patch of garden in the heart of London.

> "TASTE THE JOY BROUGHT BY A PATCH OF GARDEN IN THE HEART OF LONDON"

The creeper-clad wall at the back of the picture is the gable of my neighbour's house, to which my own corresponds. The garden bed seen on top of the hen house is 7 ft. broad. The border of greenery covering the front is the common Creeping Jenny, whilst various "carpet-bedding" plants are used, I think, to maximum effect in this debatable style of gardening art. The plants are kept carefully pinched and trimmed, and the care of my miniature Babylonian creation affords me much genuine pleasure during the summer months.—R. T. Foxlee

AUGUST 23RD, 1913

LITTLE GARDENS FOR LITTLE LONDONERS

THE QUESTION OF playgrounds is often discussed and open spaces have been provided in many parts of London, but this is hardly enough. Two years ago a society was formed with the purpose of "converting waste places in the poorer districts of London into gardens for children." The society rents available plots of land and for each site takes on a teacher – generally a lady with some training as a gardener and a love for children – and a man as a caretaker.

"IT IS PITIABLE TO FIND HOW MANY CHILDREN ARE UNFAMILIAR WITH EVEN THE COMMONEST FLOWERS"

The ground is divided into small plots, generally each about 6 ft. by 4 ft., and one such plot is given to each child for his or her very own. Vegetables such as lettuce, radishes, beetroot and cress are most popular, but flowers (particularly mignonette, cornflowers and nasturtium) are not forgotten.

The caretaker does the rougher part of the digging required and helps to keep order among the boys; the teacher instructs the children in every process of gardening, and encourages them to keep notebooks for their garden observations.

"IT IS BETTER THAN THE GUTTER"

On wet days, or when a change of occupation seems desirable, the boys make plot-stakes, string bags for carrying home their vegetables, and toys such as wooden bricks; the girls make pincushions and dresses for their dolls.

It is very interesting to see the children at work, their sharp little London faces keen with eagerness and enjoyment. Of course, not all the children take to it to the same degree. A boy may love to run around the narrow paths with a wheelbarrow – healthy exercise, but not a sign of gardening taste. Nevertheless, it is better than the gutter.

It is pitiable to find how many children are unfamiliar with even the commonest flowers. A set of boys who had been gardening for some weeks were asked the name of a foxglove. One said it was a bluebell, the second a cornflower, and the third – who refused to be prompted – said he knew it was an animal and arrived triumphantly at "fox-terrier!"

NOVEMBER 6ᵀᴴ, 1897

THE COTTAGE GARDEN

To WANDER AROUND the cottager's plot is to come upon perpetual horticultural surprises. Doubtless some order not distinctly obvious to a stranger rules the arrangement of the old-fashioned garden, for its owners always seem to know exactly where to find the required cabbage or sprig of parsley. Yet to the casual visitor, the vegetables and flowers appear as confusedly intermingled as David Copperfield considered the land and sea were at Yarmouth. Cabbages and roses jostle each other in one bed, sunflowers beam above vegetables, pinks – the old-fashioned white cloves, so fragrant but now so rarely seen in modern gardens – run riot all over the place, and the lavender bush is never wanting. Probably there is also a gnarled apple tree, or a small plum or damson of equally venerable age, whose crop is generally sold to the same good-natured local customer year after year.

"TO WANDER AROUND THE COTTAGER'S PLOT IS TO COME UPON PERPETUAL HORTICULTURAL SURPRISES"

This arrangement is not altogether without its charm, and the gardenless cottage is happily a rare, indeed almost unknown, spectacle in many rural places.

Besides its flowers and vegetables, there are certain stock adjuncts which the typical cottage garden "should never be without." The deep, roomy porch in which the tired labourer smokes his pipe on summer evenings while superintending the weeding and watering operations of the younger members of his family seems, in a way, to be more part of the garden than the house. This porch is usually covered with some sweet-smelling creeper – honeysuckle or the like – planted partly for ornament, but also with a consideration for the requirements of the bees, a hive or hives being formerly found in nearly every country labourer's garden.

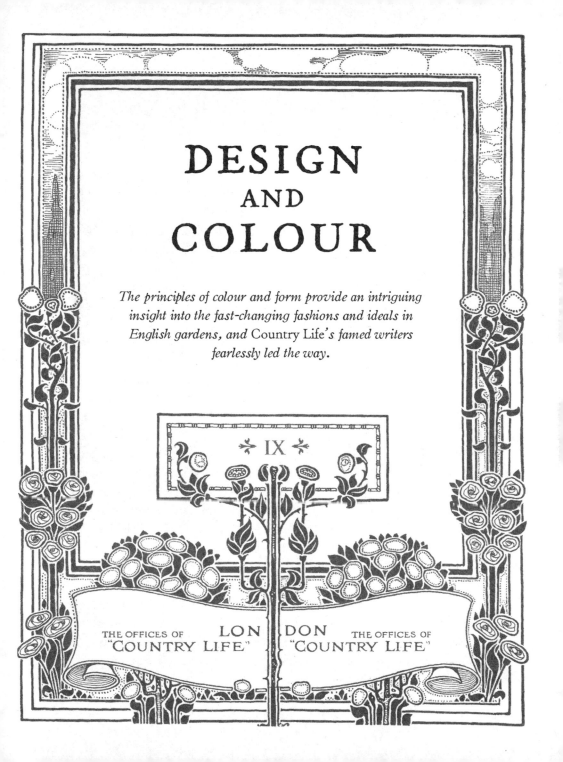

DESIGN
AND
COLOUR

The principles of colour and form provide an intriguing insight into the fast-changing fashions and ideals in English gardens, and Country Life's *famed writers fearlessly led the way.*

✦ IX ✦

THE OFFICES OF **LONDON** THE OFFICES OF
"COUNTRY LIFE" "COUNTRY LIFE"

FEBRUARY 23RD, 1929

THE FORMAL GARDEN OF TODAY

By H. Avray Tipping

THE WAR, AFFECTING our outlook and curtailing our purchasing power, has reacted on gardening, too: the most results with the least labour is now the general call.

But it must not monopolise our attention or oust that finished and formal gardening which consorts so sympathetically with the definite lines and angles of the dwelling. The wood and wilderness are right enough, but our matured taste frowns at the thought of bringing them up to the doorstep. A moderate interval where man disciplines Nature should be crossed before the greater area of her freedom is reached.

> "THE WOOD AND WILDERNESS ARE RIGHT ENOUGH, BUT OUR MATURED TASTE FROWNS AT THE THOUGHT OF BRINGING THEM UP TO THE DOORSTEP"

This view, fortunately, has so strong an attraction for us that we still find the formal garden holding its own. Existing ones have been altered and maintained, and new ones have been devised and laid out. Had this not been the case, it would have been a thousand pities, for the school of formal gardening that arose in England before the end of the nineteenth century – and was so full of vigour in 1914 – possessed in high degree the qualities of thought and reasonableness. Designers had reached the point of very carefully considering the characteristics of the intended site and, far from obliterating or ignoring them, they preserved them, made features of them and by clever manipulation of them gave individuality to their schemes. We can see that this school is still flourishing from the variety of post-war gardens, each adapted to the house it supports and the landscape it adjoins.

DECEMBER 9TH, 1922

THE GREY BORDER FOR LATE SUMMER

By Gertrude Jekyll

WHILE THERE IS still time to plant, it may be well to remind readers of the great pleasure that may be had from a well-arranged mixture of purple, pink and white dowers, with a groundwork of grey foliage. The plan shows a short section of such a border, with hollyhocks (pink and white) at the back and several bushy shrubs, each of which has a special purpose.

The sea buckthorns (*Hippophae*) are to support a clematis which is trained through and over their branches. Although they would naturally grow to something like 8 ft., we prune them to a height of 6 ft. at most and trim back the branches to the shape required. Sea buckthorn is dioecious, therefore it is best to use the male plants only as the bright orange berries of the female form will interfere with the intended colouring.

The clematis has a great dislike to having the bare lower part of its stems exposed to sun and air. If there is no growing thing a couple of

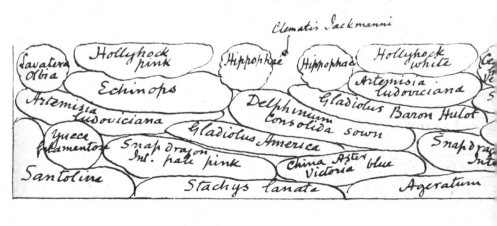

feet high that will provide some shelter, some dry bracken or anything leafy should be placed close by (long heather is excellent). It should also be remembered that they require a limy compost, unless they are in naturally chalky soil.

The *Lavatera olbia* can be a valuable bush in the grey borders, but a word of caution is necessary. There are two distinct forms of this shrub, and the one of which seed is commonly sold – I believe distinguished as *Lavatera arborea* – is not suited for the flower border as it grows too coarse and bulky. The right plant is a neat bush about 4 to 5 ft. high, and its leaves are smaller, more bluntly lobed, and rather ivy-shaped. It produces plenty of bloom of that rather low-toned pink that goes so well with grey and purple.

> "THE BRIGHT ORANGE BERRIES OF THE FEMALE FORM WILL INTERFERE WITH THE INTENDED COLOURING"

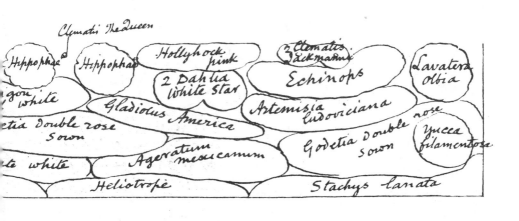

FEBRUARY 24TH, 1900

OF GARDEN MAKING

By F. Inigo Thomas

GARDEN MAKING HAS always been an architectural matter, except during a comparatively short period when the mother art was all but forgotten in our own country and the art patrons of the day conceived the brilliant idea of dispensing with all form and order. Their attitude of mind cannot fail to strike us as strange when we consider the glorious works of the past, both in England and abroad, and one can only suppose that they worked in wilful ignorance of what had been done in days gone by, or they surely would have become conscious of their lack of method. But what they did we have been content to follow, and in our haste to obtain a luxurious growth of rare

> "ONE CAN ONLY SUPPOSE THAT THEY WORKED IN WILFUL IGNORANCE"

shrubs and plants, we have lost sight of the subtle charm that lies in a fusion of well-designed architecture and symmetrical spaces with natural foliage. Above all, we have ignored the sense of fitness that a frankly designed garden bears to the architecture of the house itself.

The florist and collector is always more or less anxious that his pinetum should show examples of every known species, and that flowers, mosses and ferns from every quarter of the globe should each have a special nook in his garden. To a certain extent, the artist is with him, but his palette is much smaller and more simple. When asked to design a garden, he only asks for stone of varied textures – this he must have to make a framework – a little turf, a fair bouquet of flowers, some English yew, a box for borders, some water, and a delicate fancy or two in wrought iron. This will do. The larger background may be left to the forester, but with a plea that he will employ for the most part those trees that rear a lofty cliff of green overhead and leave broad leaf-strewn avenues amid their trunks. But this reluctance on the part of the artistic to make provision in their gardens for every known species of plant is never likely to find favour in the eyes of the nurserymen.

FEBRUARY 13TH, 1909

THE STREAMSIDE GARDEN

By Gertrude Jekyll

To HAVE WATER, whether of pond or stream, in a garden is the greatest possible gain. If the little waterway passes through a dressed flower garden, it may be tamed to take its part in the garden design in rills and pools and basins, bordered with wrought-iron and stone kerbing, and planted with such beautiful things as the Japanese *Iris laevigata* and *Iris sibirica* and scarlet lobelia. But if it passes through the outer part of the garden, or near grounds of wilder character, the plants used – many of them natives – could be the water plantain with its beautiful leaves, the flowering *Butomus* rush, the lovely water forget-me-not, the deep yellow marsh marigold, or the bright yellow *Mimulus*, so long acclimatised that we class it as a native. For foliage, consider the common bur-reed (*Sparganium ramosum*), the lady fern or the dilated shield fern. Then

> "TO HAVE WATER IN A GARDEN IS THE GREATEST POSSIBLE GAIN"

comes the pale pink Spiraea venusta, the rosy *Spiraea palmata* and the white-plumed *Spiraea Aruncus*, a native of the banks of alpine torrents.

It should be remembered that the best effects are gained by some restraint in the numbers of different kinds of plants used. If in one stretch of 20 to 25 ft. the plants are blue forget-me-not, yellow *Mimulus* and lady fern only, one can see and enjoy these lovely things to the full, and far better than if there were two or three other objects of interest besides.

SECTION

Feet 0   5   10

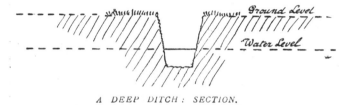

A DEEP DITCH : SECTION.

PLAN OF PATH AND
STREAM.

FEBRUARY 7TH, 1914

PLANTING A CARRIAGE DRIVE

BY GERTRUDE JEKYLL

I T IS PERHAPS best that the planting just within one's entrance gate, and from there to the house, be kept green and quiet – a suitable introduction to a bright display of flowers in the garden proper – although no one can find fault with the feeling of gracious hospitality that prompts the planting of bright flowers as an immediate and cheering welcome to the visitor. A suggestion for such a planting, in a belt on each side of the road, is shown in the illustration.

> "THE LONG-SHAPED DRIFTS AVOID THE MEANINGLESS, SPOTTY APPEARANCE SO OFTEN SEEN"

A wide grass verge should lie next to the road, and there must be a good proportion of evergreen shrubs so as to secure a well-clothed appearance in the winter months. Consider therefore, close to the entrance, some groups of green holly enlivened by the silvery stems of birches. Then might follow rhododendrons and common junipers, with pernettyas and andromedas to the front, and beyond

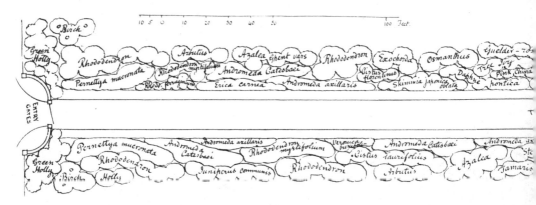

them tamarisk – a beautiful shrub that is too much neglected in general planting.

After a good stretch of shrubs of green foliage, with suitable companions of deciduous habit, there comes a region where reddish colour, both of bloom and leaf, predominates, *Rhus Cotinus* being a charming choice.

At the far end and on the opposite side, the prospect is further varied by a glow of golden foliage and yellow bloom. The shrubs are planted in generous masses, and long-shaped drifts join one group pleasantly with the next, avoiding the meaningless, spotty appearance so often seen.

DECEMBER 7TH, 1912

LESSER COUNTRY HOUSE GARDENS

By Arthur T. Bolton

THE HANDSOME VOLUME of *Gardens for Small Country Houses*, by Gertrude Jekyll and Lawrence Weaver, is a notable addition to the COUNTRY LIFE Library. From it our readers will see how far we have travelled from the Victorian Paradise which, with its laurelled demi-lune-shaped drive and shapeless grass lawn set with *Araucarias*, is at last dead.

The right of the architect to control the setting of his work is now conceded, and the strong common-sense that has controlled the cottager's garden has prevailed against the misleading naturalistic analogies of the formal landscape gardener.

In England, natural facts of climate provide us with unrivalled grass lawns, glorious flowers and a wealth of foliage that other lands sigh for in vain, and the true line of development in English gardens, whether large or small, must lie in the right display of our own resources and in laying the stress on those unique features which constitute the abiding charm of England.

For it is saddening to see the destruction of the natural qualities of a fine site by the importation, often at vast expanse, of features and material quite alien to the locale: must a pergola always take the place of the native pleached alley? If we are denied the orange groves of Sicily and the olive trees of Tuscany, are not the Kentish orchards and hop gardens an adequate equivalent?

Whilst the extended use of fountains and water effects that always come first in sunburnt and thirsty lands may be denied to us, water is one of the elements which may find a just use in the garden of a small country house, and the long series of examples in the book by Miss Jekyll and Mr. Weaver will help to a right understanding of its possibilities.

> "LAYING THE STRESS ON THOSE UNIQUE FEATURES WHICH CONSTITUTE THE ABIDING CHARM OF ENGLAND"

SEPTEMBER 28TH, 1912

THE FLOWER GARDEN AT GRAVETYE MANOR

By William Robinson

HE EDITOR TOOK a fancy to have a plan of my garden, and I willingly agreed, but desire to say a few words about plans and the harm they have done. Plans should be made on the ground to fit the place, and not the place made to suit some plan out of a book. Infinite harm has been done to the good art of gardening by the copying of old plans by designers without sympathy or knowledge of the art itself. There are books full of these plans, and any clerk can copy and suggest them for all sorts of unfitting situations. In this case I thought of nothing but the ground itself, its relation to the house, and what I wanted to grow in it.

> "ANY TALK ABOUT 'STYLES' IS ABSURD"

I am a flower gardener, and not a mere spreader-about of bad carpets, and when I had a garden of my own to make, I meant it to contain the greatest number of favourite plants in the simplest way. I did what the Assyrian king and the medieval chatelaine did: I threw the ground into uncomplicated beds, suiting the space for the convenience of working and planting, and not losing an inch more than was necessary for walks.

No plan of any kind was used, nor any suggestion sought from any other garden – all questions were decided in relation to the space. For any talk about "styles" is absurd.

One day a young lady came to see my finished garden. She had been reading one of those mystifying books about formalities and informalities and, instead of warming her eyes at my roses and carnations said, "Oh, you too have a formal garden!" Just imagine what Nebuchadnezzar or the mediaeval Lady with their small patches of gardens would think of any silly person who made such a remark instead of looking at the flowers.

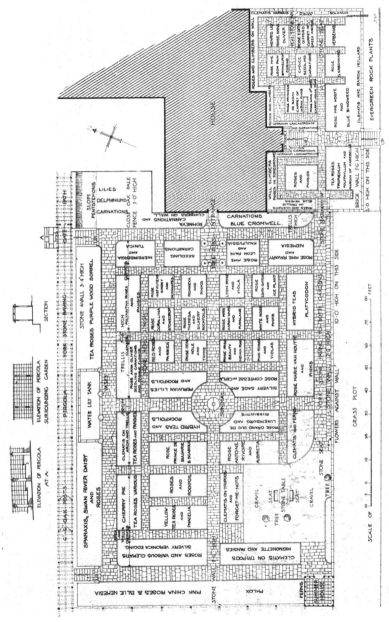

THE GARDEN PLAN AT GRAVETYE.

JUNE 10TH, 1911

THE QUEEN OF FLOWERS

BY J. H. PEMBERTON

O F ALL THE flowers of the garden, none is more popular than the rose, and it was so in the days of our grand-mothers also. At the beginning of the nineteenth century, the rose was one flower among many, and it shared the border with others with also just one crop of flowers. One short, sweet season of a few weeks' duration, and then all was over – farewell to the last rose of the summer.

"THE ROSE HAS WON ITS PREMIER POSITION IN THE FLORAL WORLD"

Not so today. Owing to the cross-fertilisation of the Provence, Gallican and Damask roses with *Rosa indica*, the rose, in about 1830, became "perpetual" and bore more than one crop of flowers (Rose du Roi, a Damask, being one of the first perpetuals).

The rise of the hybrid perpetual in early Victorian days greatly increased the popularity of the rose, and this perpetual-flowering habit has now been so improved that it is possible to have roses blooming from the end of April until late in autumn. Indeed, some of the September blooms are superior to those of midsummer.

The popularity of the rose is also due to its adaptability for many purposes. For ornamental single bushes, pillars and walls, arches and pergolas, bedding and massing, table decoration and specimen blooms, button-holes and wreaths, the rose meets all requirements, and meets them efficiently.

But the rose has won its premier position in the floral world by reason of its beauty of form, its depth of colouring and, more than anything else, its perfume. And as Sir Henry Wotton says:

You violets that first appear,
By your pure purple mantles known,
Like the proud virgins of the year,
As if the spring were all your own;
What are you when the Rose is blown?

Yes, what are violets, and indeed all other flowers, when the Rose is blown?

APRIL 19TH, 1922

A BLUE BORDER

BY GERTRUDE JEKYLL

ONE HEARS OF blue borders being planted in which there must be nothing but blue, but this uncomfortable, self-imposed restriction is entirely disagreeable. Surely it is better that a border be beautiful than that it should be rigidly and exclusively blue?

I have always found that a mass of pure blue calls for the accompaniment of something white, cream white or palest yellow. Though in general garden practice I am for putting together plants whose colours form a gradual sequence of harmony, I think that blues, on the contrary, prefer a contrast.

The display of the blue border begins in June with some bold masses of *Delphinium belladonna*, accompanied by early *Gladiolus Colvillei* ("the bride"), and with these the tall feathery spikes of *Spiraea Aruncus*, the great meadowsweet of the borders of alpine torrents, and

> "SURELY IT IS BETTER THAT A BORDER BE BEAUTIFUL THAN THAT IT SHOULD BE RIGIDLY AND EXCLUSIVELY BLUE?"

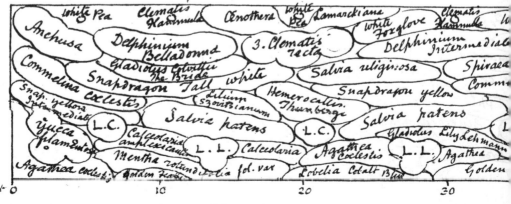

Spiraea Itaria, the double form of the meadowsweet of English stream-
sides. *Clematis recta* soon follows, with its masses of cream white bloom
so delightful with anything blue. This is a herbaceous, non-climbing
kind, and when this is over and carefully cut away, the foliage is still
of good effect in the border. Towards the end of July the *Agathea* and
Lobelia will be making a show, and the blue flowers of the later summer
are *Commelina coelestis,* whose only fault is that of closing in the early
afternoon.

The plan also shows at the back some plants of *Clematis Flammula*
and white everlasting pea. These are deep-rooting things that take some
years to come to their best, but when grown they serve to cover other
earlier flowering plants that are out of bloom.

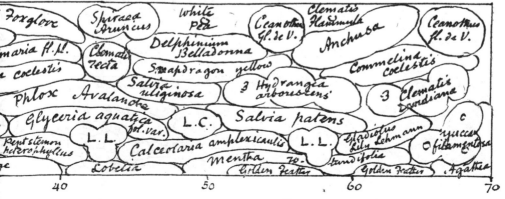

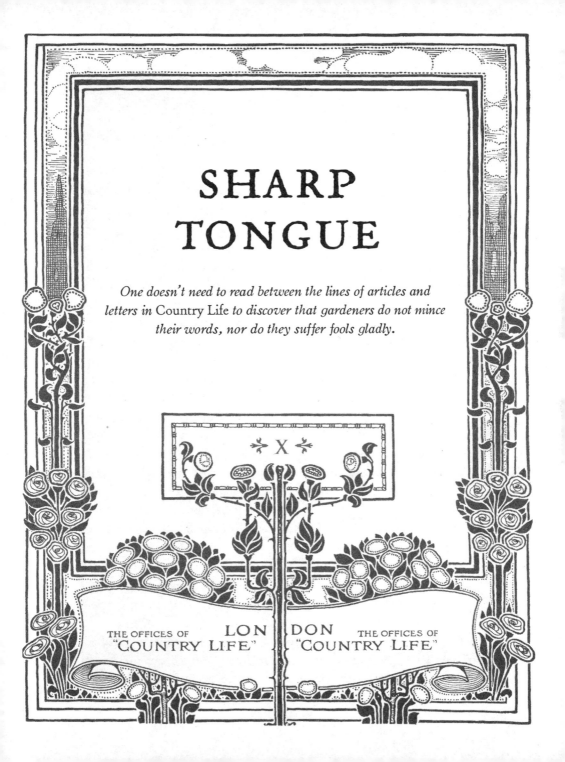

SHARP TONGUE

One doesn't need to read between the lines of articles and letters in Country Life *to discover that gardeners do not mince their words, nor do they suffer fools gladly.*

X

THE OFFICES OF
"COUNTRY LIFE"

LONDON

THE OFFICES OF
"COUNTRY LIFE"

DECEMBER 28ᵀᴴ, 1940

DIGGING FOR PLEASURE

By Stephen Gwynn

I DISLIKE "SLOGANS" because I dislike the debasement of a word which called up gallant images. I detest the idea of attempting to lead people with a catch-cry, and am furious that anyone should think me capable of being led on any such string.

> "WHEN FRIENDS ASK IF I AM DIGGING FOR VICTORY, MY INCLINATION IS TO BE RUDE"

So when friends ask, as they do, if I am digging for victory, my inclination is to be rude. For the truth is that, like a sensible man, I am digging for pleasure, finding it all the more because in the present condition it is a reasonable thing to do.

Yet the essential fact is that I enjoy the labour, for nearly all men and a great many women like physical exertion, called "being fond of exercise." The pleasure lies in bringing your strength to bear in the right and lucky way, and physical exertion which is enjoyed affects the nerves rather like a dose of alcohol.

One day our neighbour the dairyman looked over the gate and thought I had not dug deep enough – the weeds would come again. I said he was hard to please, for I had dug down a good twelve inches, and that he did not know how seriously I had been educated. Long ago, when I had a garden of the size that involves a whole-time gardener, one border went out of cultivation so I took it in hand to dig it over myself. Then my gardener came up and said that what I had done was no use as seedlings were left in, every one of which would come up again. So I tackled it again.

This time, I think with some surprise, he pronounced himself satisfied. "A labouring man would not have done it better," he said, and for the last five and thirty years, I have tried to live up to that commendation. At least I can say that I know how work should be done, although now and then when there is more than I can tackle, a very old labourer comes in to help. His work has a neatness and finish that I cannot approach and it is a pleasure to watch him, just as your serious amateur golfer enjoys watching his professional.

OCTOBER 18TH, 1930

OXFORD COLLEGE GARDENS

A Country Life *reader deplores the standards of gardening in the college gardens of Oxford.*

To the Editor of "Country Life."

Sir,—The "studious walks and shades" of the college gardens of Oxford, the union of ancient buildings and spacious lawns, trees and flowers, and the atmosphere of academic repose in which they are environed, has for years made these gardens unique. But, from a horticultural point of view, the Oxford college gardens are now behind the time and show some want of care and interest from those who are responsible for them. In Worcester College garden, for instance, one is immediately struck by the rank wild elders, overgrown and half-dead boxes, pines smothered by ivy, and *Calceolarias* planted in sunless borders among the shrubs. This garden with its noble trees and delightful lake – its margin so suitable for clumps of iris – shows a want of efficient management.

> "THE OXFORD COLLEGE GARDENS ARE NOW BEHIND THE TIME"

In fact, anyone who has a garden at all might make a deplorably long list of desirable shrubs missing from these gardens. New and charming roses could find perfect homes in sheltered corners, and is there in a college garden a single specimen of that delightful climber Mermaid, with its large wax-like and fragrant flowers and dark glossy foliage?

Appreciation of the beauty of gardens has recently increased in this country in an unprecedented manner, and all that is needed at Oxford is the same thoughtful and sympathetic care.—E. S. Roscoe

FEBRUARY 25TH, 1949

THE ROCK GARDEN STANDS TRIAL

By A. G. L. HELLYER

ROUGHT INTO FAVOUR by the able propaganda of William Robinson and Gertrude Jekyll, the rock garden has made an irresistible appeal to gardeners already in full retreat from the over-elaborate formality of mid-Victorian gardening. But now that the novelty has departed and the theories are outmoded, it may not be a waste of time to consider once again the exact place and value of rock gardens.

> "THE ROCK GARDEN IS A PRETENCE THAT CAN, AND OFTEN DOES, BECOME IRRITATING"

One criticism levelled by the "follow Nature" school is that the rock garden is a pretence that can, and often does, become irritating. This criticism does not apply to rock gardens which are entirely or mainly natural: no objection could reasonably be made to the conversion of a quarry into a rock garden, and nor can there be anything incongruous in making the best possible use of a site that naturally includes suitably stratified rock by baring more of the stone or rearranging some parts of it.

But there is a vast difference between adapting a design to suit the site and imposing upon the site something alien to it. Unfortunately the rock gardener, even one striving at a natural effect, too often achieves nothing but artificiality. In this he is at a disadvantage both to the landscape gardener, who merely adjusts Nature to suit his ends, and to the formal gardener, who ignores Nature and is frankly and openly artificial.

MARCH 18TH, 1949

IN DEFENCE OF ROCK GARDENS

TO THE EDITOR OF "COUNTRY LIFE."

SIR,—Mr. Hellyer's provocative article of February 25th, while interesting, is neither convincing nor conclusive. There has been much muddle-headed thinking, and much rubbish talked, about "natural" rock gardens. No rock garden looks natural, in the sense of seeming to be made by Nature. The very essence of any garden is that it is man-made, and all the really great gardens reflect the taste and character of the man who made them. Rock gardens have been built in the heart of the Alps, but no one would mistake them for a natural slice of the mountain, if only because the garden plants have been selected. In a truly natural rock garden, selection would be done by Nature alone, and all man-made rock gardens are and look artificial, although that is not to say that they need be ugly or seem out of place.

> "THERE HAS BEEN MUCH MUDDLE-HEADED THINKING ABOUT 'NATURAL' ROCK GARDENS"

Aesthetically, the test of a good rock garden is whether it harmonises with its surroundings, but it is fallacious to go on to suggest, as Mr. Hellyer does, that this harmony can be achieved only in, say, a chalk-pit.—E. HODGKIN

JULY 15ᵀᴴ, 1949

THE JOBBING GARDENER

By Esther Meynell

WHERE ARE THE jobbing gardeners when you need one? You may have a cousin in Somerset who has succeeded in obtaining their services, but Somerset in any case is a somewhat mythical county, associated with people like King Arthur and King Alfred and cakes whose existence is the cause of historical controversy.

Gardeners in general are a fruitful source of controversy. You may even have met one, run him to earth, as it were, and engaged him to do a little work for you on Friday mornings. But come Friday, or any other morning, he is nowhere to be seen. Probably there was a flood that day, or he had to fetch his Old Age Pension, or buy his special brand of tobacco, or support his son who was taking part in a ploughing match. There are many possible reasons.

> "GARDENERS IN GENERAL ARE A FRUITFUL SOURCE OF CONTROVERSY"

Even when Old Jobbing does arrive, he is apt to retire gloomily to the potting shed. You keep peeping from the scullery window to see if he has come out, but he stays there as firmly as a watched snail in its shell. In desperation you brew a large cup of strong tea and take it to him (you don't like to intrude on his solemn meditations without some excuse). He is not at all pleased to see you, though he gulps down the tea and proceeds to give you his views at great length on football pools, which, of course, does not help to get the onions in.

Whether your gardener is young or old, one thing is certain: he will never do what you tell him. He has his own ideas and, particularly if you are a female, can never bring himself to regard you with the charity of the pig for, as the saying goes, whereas the dog looks up to you, and the cat looks down on you, only the pig regards you as a fellow human being.

You may have an uncle who is considered an authority at Kew, and he may have given you his valuable personal advice, but it is no matter. The jobbing gardener will tell you it is "too early" or "too late" or "too wet" or "too dry" for whatever you want done.

MARCH 12ᵀᴴ, 1904

PARKS AND NURSERIES

By William Robinson

L ONDON PARKS ARE being disfigured at an alarming rate. The stiff banks now being formed, for example, are needless and sure to end in ugliness, for the practice of raising mounds for beds is against all good work in landscape gardening. It is assumed by the mound-makers that the ground is not right for their purpose, and so dumplings of earth are thrown up here and there to change the natural form of the ground. Anything uglier than the aspect of places such as Park Lane now, even in the middle of the summer, can hardly be imagined, and this costly and inartistic system is wrong in every way for our climate, for colour, or for effect.

> "ALL CROWDED TOGETHER AND DISTRESSING IN THEIR WARRING SHADES"

Last summer the plants used for colour effect in the parks were in many places a complete failure, and shocking combinations were seen, such as blue lobelia, scarlet geranium, mauve verbena, and purple and variegated fuchsias, all crowded together within an area of a few feet and distressing in their warring shades. Picturesque groupings of plants are far better.

In a northern country like ours, in which frosts occur even in summer, it is folly to trust tender plants alone and I am displeased by the adornment of the park with things grown in hothouses for eight months of the year. Nothing for the permanent beauty or good of a park can be done in a hothouse and it also gives rise to a pot-and-kettle race of gardeners, useless in the open air where they are most wanted. Some may say that the people enjoy floral displays of stiff hyacinths in the spring, lasting but a few days in our dirty atmosphere. But the answer is, give them a chance to see something better.

The permanent planting of the whole park should be considered, and we should see something better than the broken-backed elms and the commoner trees. The elm – the most dangerous, treacherous and worst of trees – is far too much seen in the park, and often surrounded by spiked rails. If we planted good trees we should have their beauty in the winter as well as in the summer instead of wasting all our efforts in making a show for a few months in one place only.

AUGUST 15TH, 1903

THE NEW GARDEN OF THE ROYAL HORTICULTURAL SOCIETY

IT WILL BE a matter of interest and probably gratification to many readers of COUNTRY LIFE to know that the Royal Horticultural Society has, through the munificent gift of Sir Thomas Hanbury, acquired a garden for horticultural experiments in the future. It is well known that the gardens at Chiswick, now a suburb of the metropolis, are useless for any serious horticultural purposes, and Sir Thomas Hanbury has been actuated by the needs of the times. He has purchased the beautiful Oak Wood garden at Wisley, comprising 59½ acres, as a gift to the great Society of which he has for many years been a member.

> "THE GARDENS AT CHISWICK ARE USELESS FOR ANY SERIOUS HORTICULTURAL PURPOSES"

The Society has been passing through a social crisis, for as well as a new garden, a new horticultural hall is also much needed – the paltry premises it enjoys at present are despicable. There has been a desperate contention as to whether the Society should purchase a garden or a hall, so through the munificence of Sir Thomas Hanbury, the Society has been relieved of embarrassment.

> "THE PALTRY PREMISES IT ENJOYS AT PRESENT ARE DESPICABLE"

The late Mr. G. F. Wilson, who spent many happy years at Wisley, would surely be happy to know that his garden, situated in the most beautiful of Surrey woodlands, will now be in such loving hands. We congratulate the Society on acquiring so famous a place for their trials and their experiments.

OCTOBER 8ᵀᴴ, 1898

PROSPECTS OF FIG CULTURE

Country Life's Editor does not spare his scorn when dealing with an early believer in climate change.

To the Editor of "Country Life."

Sɪʀ,—Many of your readers besides myself must have noticed the uncommon excellence this season of the figs, more full and luscious than I ever remember them being before. Now, Sir, there is but little doubt of the reason of this: it is a consequence of the late spring keeping back the young growth, and the subsequent warmth and sun of the late summer and early autumn, which has been more like Italy than England. There seems to be very little doubt that our climate is gradually changing: the springs are becoming more backward and the warmth of summer is coming to us later in the year. I should think it would be wise for us to pay more attention to our outdoor fig culture, whether against walls or as standard trees, than we have previously been accustomed to do – a suggestion that may perhaps be followed with advantage by some of your readers.—F. L. M.

> "WE ARE INCLINED TO THINK THAT HIS INFERENCE IS PERHAPS NOT DRAWN FROM A SUFFICIENT NUMBER OF OBSERVED SUMMERS"

[We are much obliged by F. L. M.'s letter, but are inclined to think that his inference is perhaps not drawn from a sufficient number of observed summers to warrant experimenting with figs on a large scale.
It is true that a very careful observer lately surprised us with the statement that on no fewer than ten days during September 1895 the thermometer

rose to over eighty in the shade, but we are disposed to think that such observations must extend over a considerable stretch of years before we can safely infer any permanent change in our seasons.—Ed]

MAY 19TH, 1900

THE INIQUITY OF CARPET BEDDING

A REVIVAL OF this worst form of summer gardening is now being attempted in some places. Money and labour are being wasted upon petty scroll designs as wretched as the plants used in their formation, as dragons of fearful device, or cockatoos of impossible shape, are worked upon the lawn.

> "A FASHION UGLIER THAN CRINOLINES AND BIG HATS"

Hundreds of little hothouse plants must be used in these designs, and the correct representation of the thing portrayed is maintained by weekly clipping and pinching to prevent the growth outrunning its allotted space. If those who indulge in these strange fancies can give solid reasons for their introduction into the flower garden, we shall be pleased to publish them as interesting defences of a fashion uglier than crinolines and big hats. For may we be spared a fever of scarlet geraniums, blue lobelias, dingy Alternantheras, and ill-looking Pyrethrums.

JULY 31ST, 1897

PRIVET A MISTAKE

A MORE POWERFUL, yet more monotonous, shrub does not exist than the common privet. It is obnoxious now in a twofold way: its dull, uninteresting leafage and its evil-smelling flowers. We were lately in a garden in which privet abounded and belched out its offensive odour. And no shrub is more hungry, its roots robbing the ground of nutriment for many yards.

AUGUST 19TH, 1939

THE SEASON OF THE SHEARS

To the Editor of "Country Life."

SIR,—I have seen it stated that most evergreen hedges are entirely spoiled (for man and bird) by too close planting, but surely no one would plant closer than a yard apart if a close screen is eventually wanted? No opportunity is ever lost by modern gardeners to deride the box as a harbourer of snails, etc., but has anyone really discovered a more beautiful or permanently useful division between path and border or, when established, a more foolproof one? Lonicera is a poor substitute for box or yew and far inferior in colour, and the labour of keeping it shapely is considerable – the extra cost of yew or box soon justifies itself by its increasing beauty and easy management. And why is the beautiful and protective thorn increasingly neglected and that natural substitute for barbed wire, the Honey Locust, with its stout needles 2 in. long, seldom seen? Nature has its revenge on gardeners who think they can get quality of growth by substitutes at a low price.—P. MORLEY HORDER

> "NATURE HAS ITS REVENGE ON GARDENERS WHO THINK THEY CAN GET QUALITY OF GROWTH BY SUBSTITUTES AT A LOW PRICE"

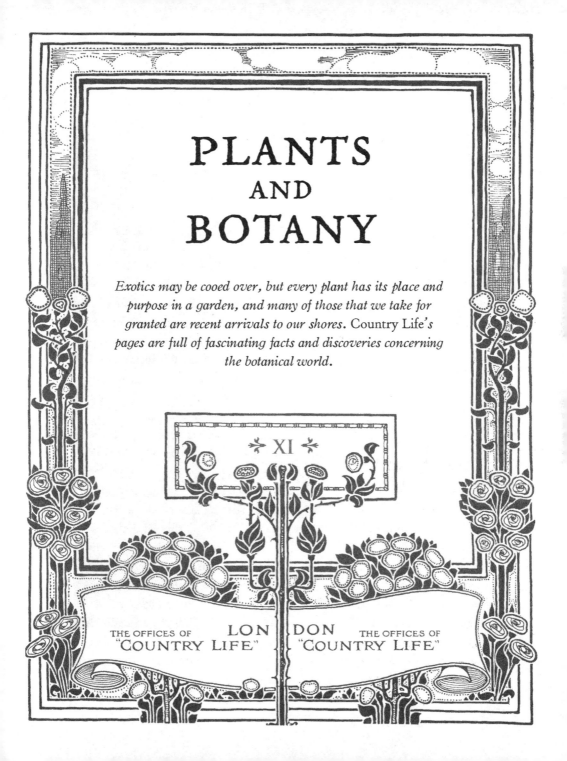

PLANTS
AND
BOTANY

Exotics may be cooed over, but every plant has its place and purpose in a garden, and many of those that we take for granted are recent arrivals to our shores. Country Life's pages are full of fascinating facts and discoveries concerning the botanical world.

❖ XI ❖

THE OFFICES OF
"COUNTRY LIFE"

LONDON

THE OFFICES OF
"COUNTRY LIFE"

SEPTEMBER 17TH, 1929

BLOSSOMS OF BROBDINGNAG

By Christopher Hussey

Karl Blossfeldt, the famous photographer of natural form on a magnified scale, is celebrated by Country Life.

A S REMARKABLE AS Gulliver's powers of observation were, he sometimes failed (as what traveller does not?) to describe just the things that we most want to be told about. He rarely showed himself possessed of an artist's eye or poet's sensibility, and this defect is particularly noticeable in his account of Brobdingnag. For what would we not give for an account of the monstrous vegetation of that country, and each of us – in childhood, if not in our maturer years – has probably found himself unconsciously trying to supply Gulliver's omission. Oh to see the miniature jungle through the eyes of the ant or ladybird adventurously threading a primeval forest of turf, clambering over grass-stalks like fallen tree trunks and disappearing into sinister recesses beneath a plantain leaf!

"THE CAMERA'S LENS IS DISPASSIONATE, AMORAL"

Now a traveller has visited this Brobdingnag of hillside and hedgerow with a camera and revealed the incredible beauty of this land that we crush beneath our seven-league boots. Using a strongly magnifying lens, Professor Karl Blossfeldt has photographed fronds of ferns as though they were bishops' croziers and shoots of a yellow aconite as large as if it was a man, and the extraordinary plates from his book *Urformen der Kunst* ("Art Forms in Nature") reveal a new and unsuspected realm of incredible beauty. Some have a resemblance to Gothic ironwork; others to a strange Oriental architecture. The common mare's tail is seen, in magnification, to look like a Congo sculpture or the Tower of Babel, and shoots of horse-chestnut resemble Red Indian totem poles, complete with a grotesque human face.

The camera's lens is dispassionate, amoral: no humanising sentiment infuses these pictures of exquisite structure with a false pathos. We see Nature austere and linear but also voluptuous, and we feel abashed at surprising her thus naked, engrossed in her passionate sequence of conception, growth and decay. Seen ten times life-size, the stamens and pistils of these pretty flowers are avid organs of fertilisation, embowered in an exquisite chamber of marshalled petals borne upon a fluted, moulded or spear-studded column above the burrowing, thirsty roots. Gulliver, perhaps, did well to keep to himself his perils among the honeyed calices and disturbing splendours of these flowers.

MAY 16ᵀᴴ, 1931

EASTERN FLOWERS IN ENGLISH GARDENS

BY THE HON. H. D. McLAREN, PRESIDENT OF THE
ROYAL HORTICULTURAL SOCIETY

SOME TWENTY-FIVE YEARS ago there died a man who was one of the leading amateur gardeners of his time, a man who grew every new plant he could get hold of and all the best old ones as well. E. H. Wilson's successors have maintained his garden excellently but added no further plants, and that garden today, though interesting, is a lesson in what we would have missed had the flow of plant introductions stood still during the last quarter of a century.

"THAT ONE PLANT WOULD HAVE SUFFICED HIM FOR A MEMORIAL FOR ALL TIME"

One would have most missed the Chinese rhododendron species, and of all rhododendrons the smaller-growing Chinese species are, in my view, the plants of the future. The plants we would have missed include the *Rhododendron orbiculare*, the *Rh. Griersonianum*, the *Rh. cantabile*, and Kingdom Ward's *Rh. riparium*.

We would be without the Chinese magnolias, too – *Magnolias wilsoni* is akin to *M. parviflora*, and both are lovely things, but I believe that *Magnolia Sargentiana* far surpasses them. The latter flowered in Cornwall this spring for the first time in cultivation, though the seed came from China some twenty-five years ago.

One could also speak, if there were space, of the Chinese birches (*Betulas ermanii, albosinensis* and *szechuanica*), of berried *berberis galore*, of *Clematis armandii* with its countless scented flowers, of *Rosa moyesii*, almost a tree, and of *Buddleia variabilis*, a little coarse perhaps but able to thrive anywhere and always gaily decked with butterflies.

And what of the lilies that have been given us in the last thirty years? *Lilium lancifolium* is one of the most superb, but it is not easy; *L. regale* flowers in two years from seed and is easy, though in some places not long lived. And for the profusion of its magnificent flowers, it is unrivalled. Indeed, if *Lilium regale* had been the only plant introduced into our gardens by E. H. Wilson, instead of the hundreds he gave us, that one plant would have sufficed him for a memorial for all time.

FEBRUARY 2ND, 1935

THE FLORAL TIME-PIECE

To the Editor of "Country Life."

Sir,—It is not everybody who realises the sequence of flowers' opening and closing, a daily wonder that, once understood, constitutes a veritable floral time-piece – the plant world's clock.

At almost every hour of the day a different plant is either "getting up" or closing its petals in sleep. Some flowers have an early rising habit, and most of them open their petals at dawn. The *Convolvulus* wakes at an unconscionably early hour – 2 a.m. At 8 a.m. the wild pink and scarlet pimpernel wake up to greet the day, and at 9 a.m. the corn marigold and chickweed rouse from their slumber. At 10 a.m. a little pink flower, the mallow, wakens and her name – Lady Eleven O'Clock – tells us the time she rises. The flowers that waken early tend to "go to bed" at a correspondingly early hour. The scarlet pimpernel, for instance, goes to sleep at 1 p.m.

> "THE *CONVOLVULUS* WAKES AT AN UNCONSCIONABLY EARLY HOUR"

Other flowers open their petals much later, at 2 p.m., 4 p.m., and even as late as 6 and 7 – the time when the catch-fly flower opens for the night. One of the laws of Nature is that the plant world needs rest just as we humans do. This is why the sweet-scented flowers that open at midnight have to "go to sleep" at noon in order to take in fresh reserves of strength for their midnight glories, displayed to an unseen and mysterious audience by moonlight while the other flowers and humans are asleep.—Hallie Eustace Miles

AUGUST 26ᵀᴴ, 1911

THE RED VALERIAN AS
A WALL PLANT

LTHOUGH NOT USUALLY regarded as a plant suitable for growing in the crevices of a dry wall, the red valerian is well adapted for this purpose. For many years a great favourite in our best English gardens, this plant was, until recently, in danger of dying out (except in a few strictly rural cottage gardens where the passing of time makes little change). During the last decade, however, several varieties with brighter-coloured flowers have been raised and it appears as though the red valerian is about to regain at least some of its former popularity. In the Round Tower Gardens at Windsor Castle, on which Sir Dighton Probyn has lavished so much loving care, this valerian has in several places established itself in the retaining walls, the plants forming imposing tufts of leaf and stem that in June are transformed into masses of rose-red flowers.

JUNE 3RD, 1933
"CACTICIANS"
By Sir William Lawrence

A RECENT ARTICLE in the *Journal of the Royal Horticultural Society* calls me a "cactician," so I will try to validate this new coinage. The cultivation of cacti is indeed a fascinating hobby for, at least at the early stage, it is the only form of gardening which demands neither a garden nor a greenhouse and can be pursued in a city as well as in the country.

Opuntia is far and away the largest genus in the cactus family. Indigenous to the New World, it was introduced into Europe towards the end of the sixteenth century. The early vernacular name "Indian fig" has given way to "prickly pear" and the *opuntia* is now divided into tunas and chollas, the former having flat stems and the latter cylindrical.

The cultivation of cacti in the open air is very popular in California, and there are fine collections at the Huntington Art Gallery at San Marino, at the McCabe Cactus Gardens at San Diego, at Santa Maria, and at Fresno. Coming nearer home, the climate of the Riviera is suitable for cacti and succulents – the gardens of the Prince of Monaco are famous. The largest collection in England is at Kew, and is raised in the Succulent House, the Sherman Hoyt Cactus House, and in two double-span pits in the frame yard. It was Mrs. Sherman Hoyt of Pasadena who arranged, at the Chelsea Show in 1929, an exhibit of South Californian cacti in a suitable environment. Not only did she present this collection to Kew, but also built a house where they are displayed against a scenic background. The Hoyt collection contains a fine example of the torch cactus (*Echinocereus Engelmannii*), which bears glorious rose-pink flowers with yellow stamens and feathery green stigma. A Cactus Society formed in England in 1898 and published the *Cactus Journal*, and in 1931 the Cactus and Succulent Society of Great Britain was formed and affiliated to the Royal Horticultural Society.

MAY 7TH, 1943

THE FIRE-FLOWER MYSTERY

BY T. C. BRIDGES

S O BOTANISTS ARE hoping that the London rocket may appear again in the bombed areas of London, as it is on record that this plant appeared in quantities after the Great Fire of 1666. But whether it is to appear from seeds which have lain dormant for nearly three centuries is as yet unknown.

The question of seed vitality has always been a hotly debated problem. Stories about mummy wheat or mummy peas have been pretty thoroughly exploded by botanists, yet there are cases of seed vitality which are perfectly genuine. Some 20 years ago M. Paul Becquerel, lecturing before the Paris Academy, spoke of his planting experiments with 550 varieties of seeds that had been preserved in the Science Academy Museum. The ages of these seeds varied between 25 and 125 years, and of them all only 23 germinated. But among those that grew were three species over 45 years old – they were all seeds with thick skins.

> "THE QUESTION OF SEED VITALITY HAS ALWAYS BEEN A HOTLY DEBATED PROBLEM"

I lived in Florida for some years and noticed that when a tract of pine-woods was cleared, pines did not grow again but were replaced by a species of oak. More peculiar was the fact that a purple violet appeared, a plant never before seen in the woods.

To come nearer home – in 1910 the Rev. Tertius Poole, vicar of Culmstock in Devon, turned a croquet lawn into a rosary. The turf of the lawn had not been disturbed for at least a century (the rector had proof of this from his oldest parishioner, aged 95, who said that his father used to mow this particular lawn). Five hundred roses were planted but in the following spring the newly-tilled soil between them was covered with splendid pansies. No seed had been sown and nor were there any pansies near by. Here it seems that the only possible solution is that the seed had remained in the soil for all these years and still retained vitality.

MAY 10TH, 1924

POPULAR PLANT NAMES OF TODAY

BY F. A. HAMPTON

The language of gardening is universal, except when it comes to common names, though the author of this article is saddened by the thought that we might not be inventing new ones.

MOST GARDENERS WILLINGLY admit the necessity of a dead language in the scientific nomenclature of plants. But a constant grumble nevertheless goes up against the official names – a grumble well enough justified since, with the exception of those beautiful and apt names such as *Daphne petnea*, *Viburnum fragrans* and *Eomecon chionanthus*, most are uncouth and cumbersome. Yet when the gardener himself sets about making names, the results are not, as a rule, delightful – a glance through a florist's catalogue tends to confirm Professor Weekley's regret that we seem to have lost our forefathers' talent for naming plants.

> "IT IS ONE OF THE HARDEST THINGS TO DELIBERATELY INVENT A GOOD NAME"

Two reasons may be suggested for this falling off. Firstly, it is one of the hardest things to deliberately invent a good name – many of the admirable old ones such as "love-in-the-mist," "ragged robin," and "naked ladies" were spontaneous creations of the moment and are the fit survivors of many that never became current. Secondly, the spontaneous creation of an apt and vivid plant name demands a certain freedom from self-consciousness and indifference to criticism. Children are often extraordinarily happy with their nicknames for flowers, but the florist has the vision of cold print to chill his imagination and the temptation to earn an easy favour by naming his latest labour after some friend or patron.

More common is the tendency to modify the already existing name: the street sellers have turned anemone into "nemony," just as our forefathers turned athanasia (via "atanesie") into "tansy." And in writing, "nemony" sometimes becomes "nenomy," probably to avoid changing from "n" to "m" and back again. It would be interesting to know whether any philologists would care to hazard "enemy" as the final form of this plant name.

A less popular modification is that of simply shortening: rhododendron may well become "rhodo," and the future of chrysanthemum seems to waver between "mum" and "chrysant." But such a violent mutilation of words has rather the appearance of a temporary makeshift, for it occurs rarely in the history of plant names.

MAY 22ND, 1910

PLANTING BAMBOOS OUTDOORS

IT IS ONLY during recent years that the value of bamboo for the outdoor garden has been realised to any appreciable extent. Few other shrubs will give such interest as a well-grown bamboo, especially if one or more of the slender-growing kinds is planted by the side of a pond or stream where its graceful growth is reflected in the water. Unfortunately, bamboos are at their worst from March till midsummer – the leaves during this period having a rather rough appearance – and this should be remembered for planting. Bamboos should, wherever possible, be grouped together in a position sheltered from the strong north and east winds which inflict more damage than severe frosts.

> "FEW OTHER SHRUBS WILL GIVE SUCH INTEREST AS A WELL-GROWN BAMBOO"

Fortunately they will thrive in almost any soil, but if a good quantity of partly-decayed leaves can be added before planting then so much the better – bamboos appreciate a rich rooting medium.

The following kinds can all be recommended for the outdoor garden in the Southern and Midland counties: *Arundinaria japonica* or *Bambusa metake*, which frequently reaches a height of 12 ft. and forms a dense mass of shoots and foliage; *A. simonii*, a native of China that grows to about 18 ft. high; *A. nitida*, a very graceful, slender-stemmed plant, 8 ft. high; and *Phyllostachys henonis*, a graceful, hardy plant, 18 ft. high and sometimes 12 ft. wide. Dwarf bamboos are *Arundinaria pygmaea*, 1 ft. high; *A. humilis*, 2½ ft. high; and *A. veitchii*, 18 in.

NOVEMBER 9TH, 1912

THE BURNING BUSH

BY SIR EDWARD THORPE

THE *Dictamnus fraxinella* ("bastard dittany," "burning bush," or "gas plant") is a herbaceous perennial found in various parts of Europe and has long been known and prized for the supposed medicinal virtues of its essential oil. Of late it has acquired interest for its alleged power of emitting, at the time of flowering, a gas or vapour capable of being ignited – creating a momentary and more or less luminous flame which, under favourable conditions, is seen to surround and envelop the whole of the stalks and flowers.

Many of the formal text-books on botany, and even some gardening manuals, contain no allusion to this peculiarity. And when it is referred to, the statements are frequently so guarded as to imply some doubt in the writer's mind as to the reality of the phenomenon. According to Dr. Hahn in Seemann's *Journal of Botany*, "the experiment was often repeated, but unsuccessfully. Some thought the observation of a flame was faulty; others that the plant evolved hydrogen or that the flowers contained etheric oil."

It was not until the hot and dry summer of 1857 that Dr. Hahn himself succeeded in getting a strongly sooting flame (accompanied by a crackling noise), and he successfully repeated the experiment during several summers, some of which were wet and cold. Dr. Hahn put the phenomenon down to the reddish glands on the pedicel and peduncle, which he believed contained an inflammable substance. And Mr. James Backhouse, also writing in Seemann's *Journal*, has noted the glands on the stem of the plant, too – he has frequently succeeded in causing the whole bush to blaze by bringing a lighted candle low down on the stem.

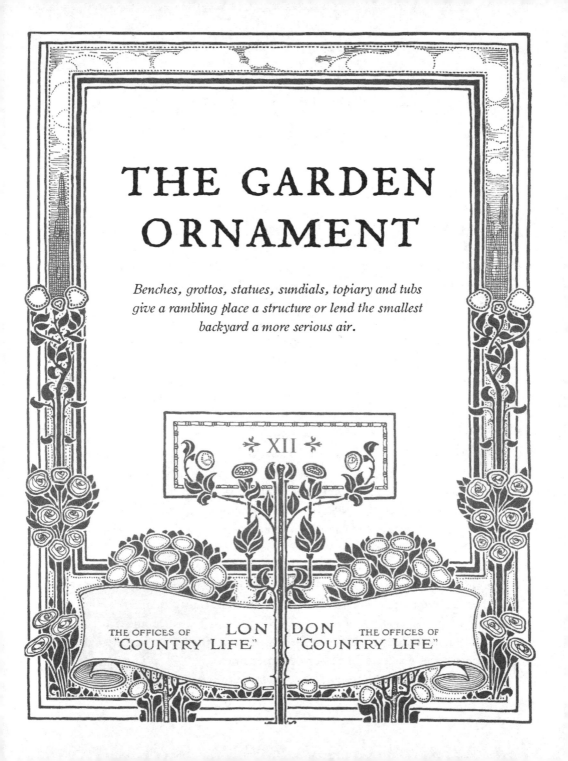

THE GARDEN ORNAMENT

*Benches, grottos, statues, sundials, topiary and tubs
give a rambling place a structure or lend the smallest
backyard a more serious air.*

✦ XII ✦

THE OFFICES OF   LONDON   THE OFFICES OF
"COUNTRY LIFE"   "COUNTRY LIFE"

MARCH 3RD, 1917

THE PAINT-POT IN THE GARDEN

By Gertrude Jekyll

Gertrude Jekyll writes, as always, with eloquence on the use of paint in the garden.

THE COLOUR OF garden paintwork does not by any means receive the consideration it deserves, and as the dry days of March are at hand, it may be well to think of the doors, gates and railings, the seats and the tubs, that will be thankful for a coat of paint, and to consider with some care what colour the paint should be.

> "THE RECOLLECTION OF THAT GARDEN BECOMES A KIND OF NIGHTMARE OF WHITE SEATS"

In some places it seems to be an inflexible law that the paint must be dead white, but often the white-painted seat becomes disastrously prominent and asserts itself with a harsh discordance in the garden landscape. One turns a corner and a white seat shrieks at the eye and commands its undivided notice, and when one goes away, the recollection of that garden becomes a kind of nightmare of white seats.

When the fact that all effect of colour is relative is ignored or unknown, such mistaken uses of good paint occur. For no paint should be of such a kind or tint that it either wars with what is near or unduly attracts to itself. If we take the case of plants in tubs, there is an unhappy convention that the tub must be a bright green and the hoops black, and the greener the green the happier the painter. But the painter thinks only of the tub, and not of the plant's colouring – it is a safe rule that no tub should be painted a green cruder than that of the leaves, and there is simply no need to paint the hoops another colour.

If it is asked what colour other than white is best used for seats, a neutral grey, such as that matched to the Spanish chestnut tree, may safely be advised. This at any rate would be safe. And for simple board seats fixed on stumps in woodland, a useful colour is that of the Scots fir bark, a warm grey. But in all painting of seats, the considerations that matter are that they should be visible enough but not unduly prominent, and that their colour should harmonise with what is near, but should never compete with it.

OCTOBER 8TH, 1921

SMALL LONDON GARDENS

BY GERTRUDE JEKYLL

An oasis in the middle of town is not only desired, but necessary, according to Gertrude Jekyll, who advises on large leaved foliage, broad lines and the effective use of stonework.

EVEN IN THE London houses of the better and best classes, there are often unsatisfactory gardens – nothing but a kind of well with buildings on every side, with walls grimed and blackened by an old sooty deposit. Such spaces have generally been neglected, but there is no reason why they should not be taken in hand and made into something that is a pleasure to look at instead of being, as now, depressingly dull if not actually an eyesore. It is all the more to be desired because, with the great increase of modern traffic, London grows more and more noisy. The rooms furthest from the roadway

"THE ROOMS ARE SPOILED BY THE DISPIRITING OUTLOOK"

are necessarily more quiet and restful but they are, at present, spoiled by the dispiriting outlook.

Recently I have been discussing this subject with Lady Feodora Gleichen, and I have the privilege of using some of this artist's sketches to illustrate some suggestions for the bettering of these small back places. The picture shows a small walled court, panelled in brick and stone. At the far end, steps on either side lead to an upper terrace with stone seats and a wrought stone balustrade, and on this upper terrace is a central wall fountain. Such an idea may be varied almost infinitely.

With regard to planting, it is well to keep it on broad lines and to have the growing things distinctly contained in stonework. By far the best way is to have a good proportion of foliage of rather large size, such as acanthus, funkia and the best of the broad-leaved saxifrages, and potted plants can be dropped in and changed as they pass out of flower. Lilies will be among the best, especially *L. longiflorum*, *L. candidum* and *L. speciosum*, and funkia, aspidistra and fern will be useful to arrange with the flowers so that no pots are actually seen.

Owners of good London houses might do a similar thing for their servants. The view from the kitchen window on to the wall of the area a few feet distant is not exhilarating, but could be improved by making it into a fern garden. Small plants of male fern may be planted, with other little plants such as London pride, musk and moneywort and the bright green tiny helxine can be planted between to form an enjoyable wall garden.

APRIL 18ᵀᴴ, 1925

SOME OLD SUNDIAL INSCRIPTIONS

By G. V. C.

A N ANCIENT SUNDIAL in an old-world garden strikes a peaceful and appropriate note and harmonises well with its environment. But it is essential that the garden where it is placed should be a fitting background. One sometimes sees, and regrets, the sight of an old sundial in the grounds of a suburban villa or a glaringly modern house; on the other hand, one often looks for it in vain in gardens where rose-clad pergolas and grassy walks cry aloud for its presence.

"GO ABOUT YOUR BUSINESS!"

How quaint some of those old inscriptions were, composed in days when there was leisure in which to pay heed to the moral which lurked in each. "Hours are time's shafts and one comes winged with death," remarks the sundial at Keir House, near Dumblane, and the following aspiration projects from the library window at Arley Hall, Cheshire:

May the dread book at our last trial,
When open spread, be like this dial.
May Heaven forbear to mark therein
The hours made dark by deeds of sin.
Those only in that record write,
Which virtue, like the sun, makes bright.

"Pereunt et imputantur" – a motto which tells us that the hours which slip by idly and unprofitably are nevertheless written up against us – is to be found on many dials, among them the Inner Temple clock at All Souls College, Oxford, and in the cathedral at Exeter. Cut in the stonework above the sundial of the Church of St. James, Bury St. Edmunds, is an injunction to the reader to "Go about your business."

About this motto, which is also on the dial in the Middle Temple, there is told a story which, if not true, is at any rate "well found." A much-occupied Bencher was on one occasion greatly irritated by the painter who was perpetually interrupting his privacy with questions concerning the inscription. "Go about your business!" exclaimed the irate Bencher and the man, taking that as his answer, affixed the words to the sundial.

It would seem that these dials were in use in Shakespeare's day, for in the "Forest of Arden" the Fool "drew a dial from his poke / And, looking on it with lack-lustre eye / Says very wisely, 'It is ten o'clock.'"

OCTOBER 14ᵀᴴ, 1929

EDEN IN TOPIARY WORK

To the Editor of "Country Life."

Sir,—The strange scene in topiary work shown in the photograph which I send you is enacted in a garden in Aborgwili, Carmarthen. In spite of the trousers worn by Adam and the quite modern, if rather unfashionable, frock worn by Eve, it is intended to represent the Garden of Eden. A very little study will show that an apple representing "the fruit of that forbidden tree," is in Eve's hand and the serpent, very insinuating in his address, is near by. Just behind Adam, at his right hand, the Angel Gabriel looks on at our first parents' fall.—P. L.

FEBRUARY 3ʳᵈ, 1940

STATUES FOR BULLETS

To the Editor of "Country Life."

Sir,—The enclosed photograph is of one of the "Sunderland Babbies" – two curious lead figures in Roker Park, Sunderland. They are said to have been brought over from Germany during the Napoleonic Wars to be made into bullets. The duty tax on lead as ore was four pounds per ton, but there was no tax on "figures of art." These are probably two of several brought over by some enterprising skipper, and either arrived too late to be melted down or were saved by some lover of art. There are two others at Beamish, a few miles from Sunderland. The style of dress is German or Dutch. The scythe, which is Flemish or Hainault, was introduced into this country in about 1840 in place of the Irish scythe-hook.— John Mossom

JULY 18TH, 1936

A GARDEN OF SCOTTISH STATUES: SCULPTURE AND TOPIARY AT FINGASK

BY E. H. M. COX

ON THE BRAES of the Carse of Gowrie, about halfway between Perth and Dundee, lies Fingask Castle, excellently situated with a view over the Firth of Tay. In front of Fingask, and among pleasant examples of local topiary work, lies the statuary. Surprisingly little is known of the curious stone figures – local tradition is even in doubt about who sculpted them. It is generally supposed that David Anderson, a native of Perth, was the sculptor, but many of the older inhabitants of the district believe it to have been Charles Spence, a well known local worthy who spent much of his spare time carving small figures out of any small boulder that took his fancy. But the figures show a skill and life-like attention to detail almost certainly beyond Spence's powers and, as far as can be judged, the figures were executed by David Anderson some time in the early 1840s.

"THE CARVING HAS BEEN DONE WITH EXTRAORDINARY FIDELITY"

The central group of life-sized statues consists of the famous Burns trio – William Nicol, Allan Masterton and Robert Burns himself. Literary scenes are also depicted: Tam and Kate from Burns's *Tam O'Shanter*, Watty and Meg from Alexander Wilson's song of that name, and the Last Minstrel from Walter Scott's poem. Pitt the Younger is also represented.

The carving has been done with extraordinary fidelity – even the ribbing and stitches on the stockings have been carefully picked out. For a long time it was supposed that the figures were made of stucco, but a broken finger and chipped corners clearly show that they have been carved out of granite. Their weight is enormous and each figure and its support have been carved out of one block.

So little is known about the figures that one's appetite is whetted for more information – who commissioned them, where did the stone come from, how were those weighty blocks placed in position and, above all, was David Anderson the sculptor? For they show craftsmanship of a high order.

NOVEMBER 24ᵀᴴ, 1928

GARDEN TUBS

To the Editor of "Country Life."

Sir,—In Country Life you, from time to time, illustrate excellent examples of garden ornaments. Is the accompanying photograph which shows one of the tree boxes, or tubs, used in the Luxembourg Gardens, Paris, of interest to you? These are the most practical garden tubs I have seen and though, for gardens like the Luxembourg, they are necessarily on a large scale, this could easily be reduced. The system of binding is so excellently good that I think we might, with advantage, copy these tubs in England.—H.

APRIL 16TH, 1932

THE ESTATE CARPENTER'S WORK

To the Editor of "Country Life."

Sir,—You often show us interesting illustrations of garden furniture. Would you care to reproduce the accompanying photograph of a home-made garden seat, taken at Allington Castle, Kent? It is the seat of Lord Conway of Allington and it struck me as being particularly good and so very much the work of a clever estate carpenter. It also fits in excellently well with the landscape. I am sure Lord Conway will not object to my sending you the photograph.—H.

AUGUST 8ᵀᴴ, 1936

BIRDS AS GARDEN ORNAMENTS

By Frances Pitt

GREAT AS IS the beauty of flowers, it is unquestionable that birds add much to the joy of a garden. At one time the peacock was practically the only bird kept in the garden but, to put it plainly, peafowl often do considerable damage. However, there are many birds which can be kept happily, and no better example can be found than Captain H. S. Stokes's collection in his garden at Longdon, near Rugeley in Staffordshire.

Amid the colour and beauty of flowers and shrubs these birds give that feeling of life often lacking where flowers reign alone. A mandarin drake among the waterside vegetation, some Carolinas between banks of flowers, and a pair of New Zealand laughing gulls on a flagged path are but a few of the many lovely glimpses that one meets at every turn.

Captain Stokes advises care in the selection of birds. His maned geese, for example, developed a taste for aubrietia and had to be sent to exile outside the garden proper, and he finds the falcated duck and most species of wigeon undesirable as they eat many young plants. Large and heavy ducks are also apt to sit on or waddle over choice plants, and geese are difficult unless there are extensive lawns, for they are apt to make a mess of the grass.

But demoiselle cranes look very

beautiful and are not bad gardeners and ditto the Stanley crane. The smaller ducks are, of course, especially suitable for garden ponds and, among the surface feeders, Carolinas, mandarins, pintails and Bahamas do well, as does the common teal, cinnamon and blue-winged teal.

> "TO PUT IT PLAINLY, PEAFOWL OFTEN DO CONSIDERABLE DAMAGE"

Reverting to the prosaic details of the keeping of birds in a garden, the duck tribe need little looking after and are simply fed on grain. Flamingos should have bread and wheat soaked in a bucket – a few shrimps from the fishmonger may be added if they need it. With regard to gulls, house scraps, bits of meat and potato, etc. will meet the case. Gulls, by the way, though delightful pets and most charming among the flower beds, need to be viewed with suspicion as they are not above varying their diet with ducks' eggs and even young ducklings. Their amusing company may be too dearly bought!

SEPTEMBER 26TH, 1931

THE GARDEN OF AN ARTIST

To the Editor of "Country Life."

Sir,—One likes to think that an artist expresses his personality not only in his professional work but in everything that surrounds him: his house, his furniture, his clothes and even his garden. Seldom, however, does one find that idea so perfectly justified as in the case of Paul-Elie Gernez, one of the greatest of contemporary French painters, who has built for himself and his family a charming home on the seafront at Honfleur amid the subjects that he delights to paint: the port, the fishing boats, the quaint sixteenth century buildings – still unspoilt – and the charming Normandy landscape.

"THE EFFECT IS STRANGE, BUT BEAUTIFUL"

Designed on a somewhat formal plan including neat gravel paths and flower beds, the garden, though open to the sea on one side, is well protected by hedges of shrubbery and walls overgrown with creepers. Some of the ornaments of the garden are remarkable, expressing, as they do, the fantastic ideas of a great artist – mermaids, dolphins and sea-monsters – in real "sea-materials" such as sea-shells, pebbles of different colours, mother-o'-pearl, marine plants, etc. The effect is strange, but beautiful.—F. Lessore

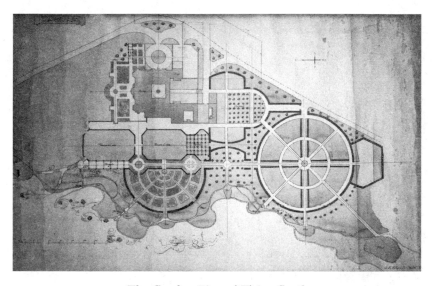

The Garden Plan of Tirley Garth

Curious Observations

A COUNTRY MISCELLANY

Already Published

'A wonderful reminder of our traditions, our country customs, that it is now, more than ever, important to guard'
JULIAN FELLOWES

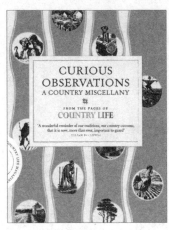

Gentlemen's Pursuits

A COUNTRY MISCELLANY
FOR DISCERNING CHAPS

May 2012

An ever-fascinating, surprising and humorous tour down the highways and byways once trodden by the Country Gent. Full of titbits from the amazing COUNTRY LIFE archive.

Letters to the Editor

WILL A MEERKAT MAKE
A SUITABLE PET?

October 2012

A 'best of' selection from the thousands of letters COUNTRY LIFE has published in its past. A real treasure trove of the humorous, the splenetic, the joyous and the just plain odd.

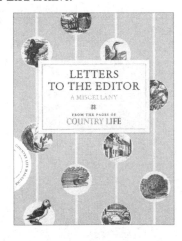

OF
GARDEN
MAKING BY
F. INIGO THOMAS